KU-546-711

MASTERING

WITHDRAWN

Printed by: MPG Books, Bodmin

Published by: Sanctuary Publishing Limited, Sanctuary House, 45-53 Sinclair Road, London
W14 0NS, United Kingdom. Web site: www.sanctuarypublishing.com

Copyright: Paul White, 2000
Sound On Sound web site: www.sospubs.co.uk

ISBN: 1-86074-289-0

basic
MASTERING

PAUL WHITE

Also by Paul White from Sanctuary Publishing

Creative Recording I – Effects & Processors
Creative Recording II – Microphones, Acoustics,
    Soundproofing & Monitoring
Home Recording Made Easy
MIDI For The Technophobe
Live Sound For The Performing Musician
Recording & Production Techniques
Music Technology – A Survivor's Guide

Also in this series

basic DIGITAL RECORDING
basic EFFECTS AND PROCESSORS
basic HOME STUDIO DESIGN
basic LIVE SOUND
basic MICROPHONES
basic MIDI
basic MIXERS
basic MIXING TECHNIQUES
basic MULTITRACKING

contents

chapter 3

chapter 4

chapter 5

introduction

One of the joys of recording music in the modern home recording studio is that the entire process can be carried out there, from songwriting and recording to mixing and mastering CDs. The mastering stage of any project can make a huge difference to the subjective quality of the finished work, and this is one reason why commercial mastering can be very expensive, but with a few basic tools and a sensitive pair of ears it's possible to produce professional-sounding CD masters at home.

The purpose of this book is to explore the techniques of computer-based mastering and editing in order to enable home enthusiasts to compile a collection of songs in the form of a finished, professional-sounding album. It's possible to produce something of similar quality to a production master CD with nothing more than a standard computer, appropriate software and a CD burner, which, as well as allowing you full control over your material, can also save you a lot of money.

introducing mastering

It's tempting to think that, once you've a mixed a few stereo tracks, all you need to do is pop them onto a CD and *voilà* – there's your album. Certainly the cheapness of CD-R (recordable CD) discs makes this an attractive proposition, but there are several processes that need to be carried out before you're ready to record a master DAT tape or burn a CD that can be used as a master for commercial production. These stages usually fall under the umbrella term of 'mastering', because their ultimate purpose is to produce a master that can be copied for commercial production. One such stage is post-production (ie further processing carried out after a mix has been produced), during which unwanted material at the starts and ends of songs must be removed, lengths of gaps between songs must be decided, and changes in level, tonality or dynamic range are implemented in order to get the various songs to sit comfortably alongside each other. All of these are a part of the mastering process, although a professional mastering engineer will often also use his or her skill and a variety of signal-processing techniques to enhance the quality of a raw stereo recording.

Editing and mastering was originally a process that was performed completely in the analogue domain, and open-reel tape was cut and spliced with the use of razor blades and splicing tape. Although the degree of editing that's possible with such mechanical means is limited, cut-and-splice editing can be used to remove unwanted material and even rearrange various elements within a song (for example, an unwanted verse or chorus can be easily removed).

It takes considerable skill to locate a suitable edit point on an analogue tape. This is generally achieved by switching off the capstan motor and then rocking the tape by hand with the machine set to Play mode so that the audio can be 'scrubbed' in slow motion. Edit points are then marked on the back of the tape with a wax pencil. A metal precision-editing block is then used to hold the tape steady as it is cut, which is usually done with a single-side razor blade that has first been demagnetised with a tape-head demagnetiser. The blade is then dragged through a machined slot cut into the splicing block, cutting through the tape at both edit points, leaving the ends precisely matched. The two ends of the tape are then re-attached with a special self-adhesive splicing tape. (Conventional tape should never be used to achieve this, because the adhesive will leak onto the surface of the tape.)

Abrupt edits are made by using a splice that cuts across the tape at 90°, while crossfades can be created by cutting the tape at an angle. However, as most recordings are in stereo, cutting the tape with simple angled splice will cause one track to fade in before another. A later development was the 'fish-tailed' edit, where the splice is cut in the form of an arrow. The geometry of this edit ensures that both tracks crossfade at an equal rate and at the same time, thus preventing image shifts from cropping up during the editing process. All three of these splices are illustrated in Figure 1.1.

The blank sections found between the tracks on an album are inserted there by the splicing in of an appropriate length of plastic leader tape, to ensure that there is no tape noise between songs. Although tape editing has since been replaced by computer-based digital editing systems, it's still a useful skill to acquire and is worth practising, if you have access to an open-reel analogue machine.

Figure 1.1: Various styles of tapes splices

Left track

Right track

A butt edit produces an instant transition across the splice

Left track

Right track

An angled edit produces a brief crossfade that occurs on one track before the other

Left track

Right track

A fishtail edit produces an equal crossfade that occurs at the same time on both tracks

labelling tapes

One of the most important things to do in order to ensure the smooth running of any recording project is to make sure that all recordings are properly documented – to do otherwise would be to risk confusion at best, and the erasure of an irreplaceable recording at worst. Fortunately, there is a standard tape labelling system that has been developed by the APRS (Association Of Professional Recording Studios), which sets out to reduce the chances of error. This labelling system is valid for multitrack and stereo master tapes, copies, clones and DAT tapes, and there's really no reason why it can't also be used with material stored on CD-R or other non-tape formats. Colour-coded labels are available via the APRS and are routinely included with blank DAT tapes, although it's a good start to simply label the box by writing on it.

essential details

In all cases, tapes and discs should be labelled with their format details: labels on analogue recordings should include details concerning tape speed, track format, noise reduction and EQ, and of course the title and date of the recording are essential. Labels on digital tapes should include their sample rates and details about the type of machine which was used to make the recording, while those on CD-Rs should indicate the type of computer with which they were made, the file formats used and the sample rates. Open-reel tapes are traditionally stored in a 'tail-out' manner, as this will reduce the amount of print through, which always occurs when tapes are stored for a long time. The tapes should be rewound before playing.

session tapes

The first tape created during a recording project is a session tape, which is generally a multitrack tape containing the first-generation recordings made during a session. In other words, it's a working tape on which material is recorded and overdubbed, and consequently it may contain out-takes as well as wanted material. The course of an album project may warrant the creation of several session tapes, and it's a good idea to store them along with their track sheets. Session tapes may be of any format, and may be either analogue or digital. With direct-to-stereo recording, the original recording is still known as the session tape and all relevant data should be recorded on the tape box or inlay card. If the tape is too small to hold a comprehensive label, it should at least be given a unique code to link it to the data held on a separate card. The APRS label is solid blue and bears the legend 'SESSION TAPE'.

original masters

When a multitrack tape is first mixed to stereo, what is produced is the original master tape. This is the earliest incarnation of the final stereo recording, and probably won't be the tape used for final production, as it may later be necessary to add EQ or edit the material. It may also contain different mixes of some material, some of which won't be used on the final production master. The APRS label is solid red, with the legend 'ORIGINAL MASTER'.

production masters

The production master is usually an edited copy or a clone of the original master on which the tracks have been organised into the correct running order and with the correct amount of spacing separating the tracks. The production master will often be equalised or processed in some other way, and because different versions may be required for different release formats it should be marked with the specific format: CD, cassette, vinyl, MD (MiniDisc), DVD (Digital Versatile Disc) and so on. The standard APRS label is solid green, with the legend 'PRODUCTION MASTER'. The label also includes space for release format details.

Many production masters are now made on DAT cassettes, which have the same 16-bit linear data format as audio CDs. A sample rate of 44.1kHz is preferred, if the machine can record at this frequency, as this means that the material won't have to undergo sample-rate conversion later in the manufacturing process. Many CD pressing plants can now work from a Red Book standard CD-R master disc, which may be more convenient to produce than a DAT master tape. (Red Book standard CD-Rs are covered in detail later in this book.)

The term 'Red Book' describes the data format used in the manufacture of commercial CDs. In addition to audio material, a CD also includes information concerning the start and end times of tracks, the number of tracks, the total playing time and other details, which is stored in a TOC (Table Of Contents) and which is accessed before the audio starts. If a CD-R is to be used as a production master, it must have all of this data in place, and configured in a way which complies with the Red Book protocol. Some software produces audio CDs that will play on a regular CD player, but they don't include all of the necessary information for Red Book compliancy. Note that production master CD-Rs should be burned in a single session (in 'Disc At Once' mode), because recording in multiple sessions will introduce errors between the tracks, which might cause a commercial CD production system to reject the disc.

production master copiers/cloners

These are recordings that are copied from the production master so that you can distribute the tape for manufacturing purposes without having to release the original production master. A tape or disc which has been copied in the analogue domain from either a digital or an analogue source is known as a copy, while a digital facsimile of a digital original is known as a clone. In theory clones are identical to their parents, although to ensure this the copying procedure must be accurate enough not to introduce any non-recoverable errors or data jittering. The APRS label is bright orange, with the words 'PRODUCTION MASTER COPY CLONE' printed on it. The appropriate box should be ticked to indicate whether it is a copy or a clone, and the label should also include all information relating to the production master.

safety copy cloners

These are simply backup copies or clones of another tape, and the label should clearly indicate the original recording from which it has been taken. The label is bright pink and is marked 'SAFETY COPY CLONE'. Again, the appropriate box should be ticked to indicate whether it is a copy or a clone.

not for production

The APRS label for any tape in any format which must not be used as a source for media manufacture is bright yellow, and bears the words 'NOT FOR PRODUCTION'.

PQ-encoded masters

This is the final version: a U-Matic tape (a type of commercial videotape carrying digital information) ready for the manufacture of a digital media release, such as a CD or a MiniDisc, and includes the coding information pertaining to the number of tracks, playing time, table of contents and other details, and is usually produced by a commercial mastering facility. The PQ-encoded master must be prepared in a specific way for each release format, so it's essential that the appropriate medium is identified on the label. The label for this stage is grey, and is labelled 'PQ-ENCODED TAPE MASTER'. The various formats should be checked in the tick boxes provided on the label, along with whether the tape is an original or a clone. Again, those who choose to master at home generally produce a Red-Book-compatible CD-R disc to be used as a production master.

media versions

Copies and clones are produced for specific purposes, such as a radio broadcast or the soundtrack to a film or video. If the tape is recorded with timecode, this should also be indicated on the label. The label is yellow and marked 'MEDIA VERSION', with tick boxes for the various media: radio, TV, film or video.

tape copying

When copying a tape, it's important to know the tape's maximum recorded level (except when making a digital clone, when the duplicate will be the same as the master tape in all respects). Analogue recordings are normally preceded by test tones at 100Hz, 1kHz and 10kHz (although often only 1kHz tones are provided) in order to facilitate setting levels, and the level of these tones should also be marked on the tape box. Correctly-recorded tones will be taped with a burst in the left channel at the start of the section, so at this point you can check that the right and left channels are around the right way. It's also a good idea to perform a few spot checks as the tape runs to make sure that the test tones relate to the recorded level. If a digital tape has been created as a production master for CD manufacture, or for some other digital format, it may not have any test tones, so it may be necessary to play the material in order to establish the level at which the peaks have been recorded.

test tones

Test tones follow a standard format: five seconds of 1kHz tone in the left channel followed by around 30 seconds of the same tone in both channels. The tone should be recorded at 0VU, and the level noted on the box. At some point the tape may be replayed on another machine, so for this reason it helps if a tone is recorded at 100Hz/0VU, followed by one at 10kHz (often recorded at around -10dB). Again, the level should be noted on the box.

When working with digital tapes, such as DAT, it's common for them to be recorded so that the peak levels fall around 2dB short of the maximum meter – or FS (Full Scale) – reading. It's always a good idea to record a couple of minutes of silence at the start of the tape, which is that part of the tape most prone to errors. If a continuous test is required for purposes of calibration, a nominal level of -14dB FS (1kHz) is considered acceptable, and once again this figure should be noted on the label. At least 30 seconds of silence should be recorded at the end of the tape before it's stopped.

mastering overview

There are now many potential formats on which a recording can be released, including CD, MiniDisc, DVD and soundtracks for films and videos, and a number of surround formats are also emerging. The most popular consumer formats are CD, MiniDisc and cassette, although vinyl is still a viable option, especially for specialist dance music. DVD audio is clearly the next big thing, while DCC (Digital Compact Cassette) has proven to be largely unsuccessful as a consumer format.

manufacturing

The aim of this chapter is to present an overview of the various processes that take place between the completion of a mix in the studio and the manufacture of a particular format from that recording.

Once the session tape (which is usually either an analogue or digital multitrack tape) has been mixed down to stereo to produce an original master, a production master must be made. The original master (or masters) will invariably contain out-takes of unwanted material, and probably all of the material will be recorded in the wrong order and with the wrong gap lengths between the songs. It may also be necessary to adjust the relative levels of some of the tracks, and at this stage it's also common practice to add further equalisation and/or compression. All of the stages of manufacture that occur between the production of the original master tape and the recording of the production master fall under the general heading of mastering.

digital formats

Most home studio owners either use DAT or CD-R to record their stereo mixes. During the mixing process, it's important to record at a level as close as possible to the digital peak shown on the recorder's meters, and if it's available the 44.1kHz sampling rate setting should be used. When working with a DAT machine that has a fixed sampling rate of 48kHz, the company who produce the CD master tape for you should be able to handle the necessary sample-rate conversion. However, it's important never to mix two or more sample rates on one tape or set of tapes – you could end up with part of your album playing back at the wrong speed. CDs are always manufactured to perform at 44.1kHz, so if you're going on to create your own Red Book production master at home, and your DAT machine only records at 48kHz, then some kind of sample-rate conversion is essential. Fortunately, most serious editing software is capable of converting sample rates, and even if you come across a program that isn't you can usually make a 44.1kHz recording from the analogue outputs of your DAT machine without experiencing any noticeably loss in quality.

When recording DAT production masters, be careful when using the Auto ID mode, as in this mode a new track ID is created when the audio level exceeds a certain threshold. Auto ID senses the presence of the programme material before writing the ID, and consequently the first notes of songs are at risk of being clipped. Because of this, it's a good idea to manually erase any Auto IDs already on the tape and write in new IDs half a second or so before the start of each track. Also, a gap of two seconds should be left after the first ID and before the start of the first track. This is particularly important in the manufacture of CD-R copies, as most stand-alone CD-R recorders take a short time to move into Record mode after detecting the first track ID.

Avoid recording music on the first or last minute of a DAT tape, and always record silence before and after the programme material – digital tapes contain subcode information, and it's important that this starts before the recording and continues for a while after it finishes. To create a gap, don't simply run the tape in Play mode, as this will leave a section of tape with no subcode.

hard-disk editing

Most commercial and semi-professional mastering is carried out with a hard-disk editing system of some kind, and most project studio owners will choose to use a computer-based system because they will probably already have a suitable computer in their studio. The requirements and operation of such a system will be covered more thoroughly later on in this book, but it's useful to have a general overview of the process.

Computer-based systems have the advantage that individual tracks can easily be 'topped and tailed' to remove count-ins and other sounds that occur directly before the music starts, and they can also edit out any unwanted sounds at the ends of tracks. Although this can be done by splicing analogue tape, a computer system can do it more accurately, as the audio waveform can be seen as well as heard. Also, on a computer it's a simple matter to undo any edits that don't work out.

It's also often possible to rearrange the various sections of a recording (for example, in order to remove an unwanted chorus or to shorten a solo). The stereo recordings can be matched tonally with the application of additional compression and/or EQ, and it may also prove necessary to perform level changes so that the tracks sit comfortably alongside each other. Although it's possible to use hardware sound processors to do this, there's a lot of editing software on the market that is equipped with this function. It's not enough to simply set the same peak level, however, as this makes songs that should be quieter sound too loud.

Fortunately, it's fairly easy to make these adjustments by ear. Fade-outs can also be added at this stage – something you can't do by splicing analogue tape.

Once the tracks have been arranged in the right order, the gaps between them must be adjusted so that the amount of space between the songs feels right, and the edited material is then either copied from the hard-disk system to a stereo tape machine (ideally a DAT machine) or it's burned onto a CD-R with software that complies with the Red Book standard. At this stage, embedded codes can be added to identify individual songs, which helps when trying to track copyrights.

production masters

When making a production master for vinyl or cassette there must be a gap between the two sides, and the playing times of the two sides must be calculated to be as equal as possible. As a rule, side one of an analogue cassette is usually slightly longer than side two so that, when the tape is turned over at the end of side one, side two is ready to play.

A full listing of the songs arranged by title, start IDs and playing times must accompany the production master, and this sheet should include full details of the recording format (such as the sampling rate) and, ideally, the type and model of machine that was used to record the tape.

Cassettes can hold a lot more material than a CD; most CDs offer a maximum recording time of 74 minutes (although it's possible to record up to 80 minutes), and you should discuss your requirements with the manufacturing company if you intend to record any more than this. For other formats, including vinyl, you should consult the manufacturer before producing the production master in order to find out the maximum playing time that can be accommodated.

commercial production

If you're planning to release your material only on analogue cassette, you may need nothing more than a copy or a clone of the production master DAT tape or an audio CD-R. Unfortunately, this isn't the case if you're aiming for a CD release, in which case there are two more stages to negotiate: the CD master tape and the glass master. However, if you can produce a Red Book standard CD-R you can bypass some of the processes involved in CD mastering and save a little money. Similarly, if you're going to add either MiniDisc or DVD to your release formats you'll need to speak to the manufacturers to find out what you need to do to meet their requirements. MiniDisc is a little different to the established formats insofar as a form of data compression is used to reduce the amount of digital data to around a fifth of that on a conventional CD or DAT.

When mastering a CD, the production master tape is arranged with no gap between the two sides of the album and has a total playing time of less than 74 minutes, including gaps. The factory will require a fully-prepared CD master tape, which is most often handled by a specialist mastering facility and involves copying the production master DAT to a U-Matic tape. This tape is timecoded, and has the necessary PQ (pause and cue) code information added to it so that it complies with the Red Book standard for CD manufacture. This additional information is used to create the table of contents on the finished CD, to enable a CD player to locate the tracks. A track title and times sheet will also be produced at this time for the CD manufacturers, and this is usually made by the same company that produces the CD master tape. Once again, you can miss out this stage entirely if you can produce a suitable CD-R master for yourself.

Some mastering facilities can make a reference CD from the CD tape master. This is a relatively cheap job, and the small investment involved is worth it for the peace of mind you have in knowing that the finished product will turn out as you expected it. A one-off CD-R is better than nothing if a proper reference CD is unavailable, although the track start times may not accurately reflect those which appear on the finished product.

Incidentally, the falling cost of low-volume CD-R duplication makes this a viable alternative to conventional manufacture for small-quantity runs of discs (250 or less). These may be made directly from a production master tape, which will save you the cost of having to have a CD master tape produced. You should be aware, however, that not all CD players will play CD-R discs, as they have different optical characteristics to those of pressed CDs, although most will play CD-Rs without difficulty.

glass masters

At the CD pressing plant, the CD tape master is played into a glass-mastering machine, which uses all of the special coding on the tape to determine the timing and table of contents of the final CD. After the data has been transferred to the glass master (which is so called because it's essentially a glass disc, used to carry the light-sensitive surface, which is imprinted with digital data by a modulated laser), the disc is plated with nickel to make a mechanical stamper, similar in concept to that used to stamp out vinyl records.

During the manufacturing process, the reflective part of the CD is stamped out in aluminium and then sandwiched between layers of transparent plastic, which protect it and make it rigid. A special, quick-drying ink is used to print labels directly onto the pressed CD, and these may be printed in any number of colours. You should consult the manufacturer over what form the original artwork should take. Some manufacturers will offer a complete package, designing body and sleeve artwork based on your sketches and photos, which can be useful if you're unsure how to produce artwork yourself.

The manufactured discs are then automatically loaded into plastic jewel cases, along with inlay cards and booklets. If you haven't gone for a package deal, these must be provided before the manufacturing stage. Not all cases take exactly the same size inlays, so it's a good idea to ask the manufacturer to send you a sample jewel case.

brokers

An alternative approach to having your CD produced is to negotiate a package price with a broker, who will handle all aspects of production, including the various mastering stages, printing and packaging. However, don't assume that everything will proceed smoothly, and check at every stage of the process. You should also make sure that there are no hidden costs before signing the deal; companies quoting attractive prices for CD manufacturing often don't include essential services, and processes such as the production of the CD master tape, glass mastering and printing are all priced as extras. Realistically, a minimum production run of pressed CDs is around 500, and the most cost-effective run is 1,000 or more.

If at all possible, try to use a recommended broker because, as in all areas of business, there is a vast difference in quality between the best and worst companies, even though they may offer ostensibly the same service.

vinyl

Vinyl records are produced using metal stampers, which in turn start life as a pair of lacquer masters, one for each side of the record. These are originally cut from blanks with a special record-cutting lathe, and then taken to the record manufacturing plant, where they are made into stampers. These stampers (known as factory masters) are made into lacquers in a process which involves electroplating.

The actual record labels are printed on paper using special heat-resistant inks, and most record plants have the facilities to arrange the manufacture of these. These labels are attached during the pressing process, and after the records have been trimmed of any waste material and inspected they are then placed in their sleeves. Inner sleeves are often an optional extra, so you should discuss sleeve requirements with the factory when agreeing on the price. As with CDs, the minimum practical quantity of records to be manufactured is several hundred.

compact cassette

The practise of manufacturing cassettes from a production master is largely different to making CDs and vinyl, as there are a number of methods available.

high-speed copying

Cassettes may be made from a production master tape, ideally in DAT format. During high-speed copying, the production master will normally be copied onto a special analogue machine which is designed to work at high speeds. The recording is made on cassette tape, which is stored on large reels (known as 'pancakes') and is wound into empty cassette shells after recording.

This procedure offers the advantage that the tape can be cut exactly to the desired length, and the copying process is not compromised by the mechanics of the cassette shells.

As a rule, both sides of the tape are copied at the same time, and unless you tell the manufacturers otherwise the recordings will be laid onto tape using Dolby B noise reduction. You will have a choice of having your cassettes made out of either standard Fe tape or Type II tape (also known as chrome equivalent), although which type you choose will depend on your budget. Standard cassette shells are available in either black or white.

In some duplicating plants, solid-state memory stores have now replaced high-speed tape in the mastering process, and in theory these produce less degradation in audio quality. Essentially, the entire album is loaded into a large digital memory, in real time, and then clocked out at high speed during the copying process.

real-time copying

Real-time copies may be made directly from a DAT source, in which case the destination cassettes are usually pre-loaded with tape. This means that you have less flexibility with regards to playing time, but this process has the advantage that it becomes economically viable to produce smaller numbers of cassettes.

high-speed tape-to-tape copying

The least satisfactory method of cassette duplication is the high-speed tape-to-tape system, in which the material on a cassette master is then laid onto blank, pre-loaded cassettes. The tape guides in cassette shells don't work particularly well at high speeds, which leads to inconsistencies in the recording quality. Also, the fact that the production master must first be copied to cassette means that there is a further stage of the duplication process in which audio degradation may occur.

labelling cassettes

Cassettes may be labelled with printed slips of paper, or the printing may be done directly onto the cassette shell. This latter process must be done during the duplication process, and it's only worth doing this when working with runs of several hundred or more, because making the special printing plates is quite an expensive process. As a rule, using paper labels will allow you more scope in the use of colour and design.

packaging cassettes

Cassettes are normally delivered in transparent library boxes, and the folded inlay cards are generally printed separately. These may then be inserted by hand if the number of cassettes is small. For very small runs, it may be worth employing a colour photocopying bureau to copy the original artwork, or you could even print your own inlays on a colour inkjet printer.

chapter 3

signal processing

The previous two chapters provide an overview of the various stages through which a stereo master recording might go before being considered ready for production. Many of these are fairly routine – level adjustments, topping and tailing and gapping, for instance – but there are also many artistic decisions about the material that must be made, and these may necessitate the use of additional signal processing.

One of the problems faced by many users of home studios is that most have monitoring environments which fall a long way short of being perfect, and this in turn may result in the production of mixes which may still require further tonal adjustment. In order to perform this job successfully, at the very least you'll need a good parametric equaliser and a monitoring system which you know is accurate and with which you are used to working. Most mastering is carried out in the digital domain, and for this reason an analogue equaliser shouldn't be used. That said, however, some of the more esoteric tube models can inject a little of their own personality into a mix. It's important to have access to a good equaliser, whether analogue or digital, hardware or software. Cheap equalisers may offer a lot of facilities but they seldom sound accurate, whereas a high-quality equaliser will enable you to make quite significant tonal adjustments without the material sounding unnatural or overprocessed. Equalisation may be needed simply to compensate for the inaccuracies of the monitoring environment in which the mixes were made, but it may also be needed to match up the sounds of tracks which have been recorded or mixed at different times.

common mixing problems

On mixes carried out in rooms equipped with near-field monitoring systems or acoustic problems, the most serious errors usually crop up at the bass end of the audio spectrum, resulting in a master that has either too much or too little bass.

At the high-frequency end of the spectrum, however, the problem is often lack of brightness or detail, especially if the recording was made with an analogue multitrack machine and several bounces were involved. It's tempting to simply turn up the high end using a shelving equaliser, but this will also bring up the noise level and may not produce the required result. It's sometimes better to identify those high-frequency sounds that need help and then use a parametric EQ or sweep mid to lift these a little. Harmonic enhancers may also be used to accentuate high-end detail, but I can't emphasise too strongly that enhancement needs to be carried out with restraint, as it's very easy to make a mix sound overprocessed or harsh.

dynamics

Some producers like to compress their final mixes while others claim that this always makes things worse. The truth is that it all depends on the type of material being mixed, and if you want to maintain a kind of high-energy feel then a few decibels of compression can help enormously. Also, compression can also help to knit together the various component sounds within a mix. Soft-knee compressors seem to give the smoothest results on complete mixes, and if you can find a model with an auto attack/release option you may find that this works better than setting up a fixed attack/release time. Remember, however, that compression will also bring up noise during quiet sections.

Limiting is also immensely useful at the mastering stage, because very often you'll have a few peaks of a really high level and short duration which force you to keep the average signal level low in order to avoid running into clipping. Because of the brevity of these peaks, they can often be limited quite severely before any audible difference is evident, but this must be done with a limiter equipped with very fast attack and release times. On a good mastering limiter it's usually possible to pull down peak levels by at least 4dB without altering the sound, which means that the average signal level can be increased by the same amount.

normalising

Hard-disk editing systems allow the user to normalise entire audio files or sections of files. Normally individual songs would be normalised, and all this process does is identify the highest peak in the selected region and then increase the gain of the entire file by exactly the right amount to ensure that this peak is the maximum digital level (or some lower level, if specified).

Before normalising a mix, there are a couple of points that you should remember. Firstly, you should never normalise if you still have any processing left to do, unless you've left yourself a little headroom (by normalising to peak of -6dB, for example). If you don't leave any headroom and later perform some other process, such as apply EQ, you may increase the signal level further, which could lead to clipping. Even an EQ setting that produces only cut can still increase the signal level slightly, for the simple reason that you may end up reducing the level of some frequency components that were previously cancelling out peaks at other frequencies. Apparently, this is also true when converting sample rates, because of the filtering involved.

Secondly, even if you've done all your processing, it may still be a good idea to normalise to a decibel or so below the maximum peak level. Clipping may also occur when a normalised signal is passed through subsequent digital systems, such as oversampling DACs. In practice this source of clipping rarely causes audible problems, but why not be a perfectionist if you have the option?

dedicated mastering hardware

A number of companies now manufacture outboard processors designed specifically for mastering. These generally feature both digital and analogue I/O, and usually include parametric equalisation, limiting and compression, along with functions such as tube emulation, dynamic equalisation, de-essing and stereo balance/width control. The best of these units split the audio into three or more frequency bands before they apply dynamic control, which reduces any audible side-effects when processing complex mixes. For example, a three-band compressor will control the level of bass sounds, such as kick drums, without causing a dip in the level of mid and high frequencies at the same time. With a conventional full-band compressor, there's always the problem of high-energy bass sounds modulating the level of mid- and high-frequency sounds.

These mastering units may also include a variety of options for noise-shaped dither – which reduces the bit depth of high-resolution recordings – and an automated facility for creating fade-outs. These devices can be used either after editing is complete or when material is transferred from a DAT or CD-R source to the computer to be mastered.

signal resolution

Some resolution is lost every time the level of a signal is manipulated in the digital domain. For example, if EQ is added the signal level will probably also increase, so the overall is then scaled down to so that it doesn't take up any more space than the original number of bits. The practical outcome of this is that low-level detail may suffer if a signal goes through several stages of digital processing, which could cause reverb tails to become less smooth or the stereo image to become blurred.

This problem may be overcome by initially working with more bits than necessary. This is why 24-bit mastering is sometimes used in CD production, even though CDs are only 16 bit. In 24-bit mastering, when all of the processing has been completed there should still be more than ample resolution, and by applying dither when the signal is finally reduced to 16 bits (to producer the CD master) low-level details will be preserved much more accurately. At the time of writing, there are few 24-bit DAT recorders available, although it's possible to master onto two tracks of a 20-bit ADAT or something similar and then transfer that data to a computer over a suitable interface.

Dither effectively adds a very low level of noise, so the signal-to-noise ratio suffers slightly while low-level distortion is reduced. A more sophisticated way of implementing dither is the practise of noise shaping, which is mathematically designed so that the components of the additional dither noise appear at the high end of the audio spectrum, where the human ear is relatively insensitive. Many software editing packages include a dither function as standard.

noise

Good recordings shouldn't have too much noise in the first place, but recordings made in home studios will often have some audible noise on them during pauses or quiet passages because of the use of budget effects, noisy synths and problems with ground-loop hums. This noise can be reduced greatly by making sure that each track is completely silent until the music starts, and this is something that can be easily accomplished with a hard-disk editor. If you're splicing analogue two-track tape, this simply means that you have to make sure that the splice occurs just before the song starts. The best way to identify this point is by manually rocking the tape over the heads and marking the back of the tape with a wax pencil to show you where to cut.

Eliminating noise before the start of a song is a great deal more straightforward on a hard-disk editor, because it's possible to see the waveform of the first sound in the song, and it's a simple matter to select the appropriate area and then using the Silence command to replace it with digital silence. At the end of the song, it's also possible to perform a digital fade-out at the tail end of the natural decay of the last sound, so that the song fades into true silence rather than a low-level hiss. This topping and tailing was covered in chapter two.

However, the noise is more difficult to eliminate if it occurs during the track, and it's usually necessary to install specialised digital-noise-removing software to tackle a prominent noise problem effectively. Less severe noise can be dealt with in the analogue domain with a single-ended noise-reduction processor, although I wouldn't recommend using one of these for serious mastering because they often produce audible side-effects. These units work by monitoring the level and frequency content of the input signal. When a low-level signal with little or no high-frequency content is detected, a variable-frequency low-pass filter moves down the audio band to filter out the noise. The filter obviously has some effect on the wanted signal, and so the trick is to configure the unit up so that it only has an effect on very low-level signals. The bypass switch can be toggled in and out so that you can hear if the sound quality is suffering, and you can then adjust the threshold level accordingly.

The operation of most software noise-removal systems relies on a bank of filters, each of which covers a very narrow part of the frequency spectrum. When the signal in a particular frequency band falls below the noise threshold, an expander kicks in to mute the signal. This happens over many independent frequency bands, and so it's quite possible to eliminate the noise

basic mastering

with the expander in one part of the spectrum, leaving the other parts unaffected.

The most basic noise-reduction systems analyse and 'learn' a section of recording which consists entirely of noise immediately before the start of a song. The system then refers to this noise spectrum to set the correct threshold for each of the multiple expander bands (although the user can define these parameters by hand if necessary). In practice, such systems are good for between 5dB and 8dB of noise reduction before any serious side-effects become evident, and although this doesn't look like much on paper it can make a huge difference to the subjective sound. Note, however, that overprocessing can cause the noise to take on a ringing or chirping character as frequency bands in different parts of the audio spectrum turn on and off.

The more advanced noise-removal programs continuously evaluate the noise in the presence of signal. This is better in situations where the level and character of the noise changes during a mix, which often happens if faders are being adjusted and tracks muted. These programs generally allow a greater improvement in the signal-to-noise ratio before side-effects become evident.

artistic considerations

When compiling an album, there are artistic as well as technical decisions to be made. The relative levels of tracks need to be balanced so that they sound good together – if all the tracks are simply normalised individually, a quiet ballad will sound much too loud if heard next to a heavy rock track. The only possible way of finding the right balance is to use careful judgement, but a good tip is to make sure that the vocal levels sound similar from track to track. Also, an old trick used by many sound engineers to identify any level problems is to listen to the music from outside the room. Any problems should be evident as one track plays into another.

A similar problem occurs if tracks are being used which have been recorded at different sessions or even in different studios. Should they sound different, or should they be EQ'd so that they all sound similar in tonal character? Again, this is up to the individual, but it's amazing how recordings of the same band can sound completely different.

Judging the length of the gaps between songs is also an art in itself. This gap is usually between two and four seconds, but this figure depends on whether the previous track stops abruptly or fades out gradually, as well as on the mood of the two songs. Fortunately the correct gap is usually pretty obvious, and I've found that, even if several people are involved in a session, the chances are that they'll agree on the correct length of the gap to within half of a second. For most material, a gap of around two or three seconds is usually a good place to start.

precautions

Make sure that you always make a backup copy of your master tape or CD-R before sending it away for duplication. You should also supply the duplicating plant with fully-documented details of the timings of tracks and tape locations of your material.

sample rates

It's important never to mix sample rates on a DAT, because most digital editing systems will simply swallow all of the data at a single sample rate, which will cause noticeable errors in speed on some tracks. Most clients, when asked the sampling rate of their DAT tape, will probably respond with "What's a sampling rate?" One way around this is to patch a hardware sample-rate converter into the input of the system so that, if a non-standard DAT tape is presented, the material will be automatically converted to 44.1kHz as it is loaded onto the hard drive.

There are other potential pitfalls involved when trying to edit a DAT tape which includes material recorded on a Casio or an older Tascam portable DAT recorder. These two machines use pre-emphasis to record material, which applies a significant amount of top boost to digital data during recording, which is filtered out again when the tape is replayed in order to keep noise to a minimum. If tapes made on these machines are transferred into an editor that can't recognise and deal with pre-emphasis, the emphasis flag is stripped out of the data stream and the result is a horrible, toppy-sounding master.

One way to get around this is to load in the sound via the editing system's analogue inputs, but the EQ setups are available on some software-based equalisers can be employed to de-emphasise a recording that has been loaded in the digital domain. This isn't a particularly common situation, but it pays to be aware of it.

practical mastering techniques

It's important to understand that there's a huge difference between what a professional engineer can achieve in a top commercial mastering suite and what the average project studio owner can do for themselves. Even so, as more computer-based mastering tools become available, it's quite possible for home studio users to achieve some very impressive results with relatively inexpensive equipment, as long as they have reasonably accurate monitoring equipment and a discerning ear.

Some people think that mastering simply means compressing everything to make it sound as loud as possible, but although it's true that compression can play an important role in mastering it's only one piece of the puzzle. The most important tool by far is the ear of the engineer, because to master successfully each and every project must be approached differently. There is no standard blanket treatment that can be applied to all material in order to make it sound more produced.

tools of the trade

Every mastering engineer has his or her own idea of what the best tools are for the job, but if you're just getting started I'd recommend that, as well as a good parametric equaliser, you try and obtain a good-quality compressor/limiter and perhaps an enhancer, such as an Aphex Exciter or an SPL Vitalizer. You will also need to have an accurate monitoring environment, equipped with speakers which have a reasonable bass extension.

To edit accurately you'll need some form of computer editor that can handle stereo files, and ideally you'll have a CD-burner connected to your computer. The computer's audio interface should ideally have digital inputs and outputs, although if you're using external analogue processors you'll probably be using analogue inputs, in which case these will also have to be of a particularly high quality. A professional engineer may start off with a 20- or 24-bit master tape or a half-inch analogue master, but in the home studio most material is recorded on 16-bit DAT. This isn't a problem for most pop music, as long as you proceed carefully and start out with a tape that has been recorded with the peaks close to DFS (Digital Full Scale).

Most mistakes are due to overprocessing, and the old adage "If it isn't broke, don't fix it" applies perfectly well to mastering. Don't feel that you have to process a piece of music just because you can; you might find that your master ends up sounding worse than the original material. If you're a newcomer to mastering, here are some tips that I've picked up over the years which you may find useful.

- Handle the endings of fade-outs in the computer editor wherever possible, rather than with the master tape that was faded while mixing. The computer will not only provide more control but it will also fade out any background noise along with the music, so that the songs ends in perfect silence.

- Editing on DAT is very imprecise, so when the material is loaded into the computer (which is best done digitally, if at all possible), use the Silence function to clean up the beginnings of songs and erase any count-ins, string squeaks, talking and so on. Use the waveform display to make sure that you silence right up to the start of the song, but be careful not to clip it. As a rule, endings should be faded out rather than silenced, because the sound produced by most instruments ends with a natural decay. When the last note or beat has decayed to around 5% of its maximum level, start to fade the material. The fade-out should be around one second long, and the song should finish in complete silence. You can still try this if the song already has a fade-out, although it may be a good idea to set a slightly longer fade time. Listen carefully to make sure that you aren't shortening the tails of any long reverb or making an existing fade-out sound unnatural.

- Once you've decided on a running order for the tracks on your album, you'll need to match the levels. This doesn't simply mean that all of your songs should have the same level, because this will simply make any softer ballads seem very loud when compared with more powerful songs. The vocals are often the best guide to a well-matched song, but ultimately it's just a matter of what sounds right. Your computer will be able to access any part of the album at random to compare the subjective levels of different songs, so use this function and pay particular attention to the levels of the songs on either side of the one on which you're working. Poorly-matched levels mostly show up in the transition between one song to the next.

- If the tracks were recorded at different times, or in different studios, they may not sound sufficiently consistent to sit together comfortably on an album without further processing. A little carefully-applied EQ will often improve matters, but you'll need to use a good parametric equaliser (either hardware or software) to ensure that you don't make matters worse. Listen to the way in which the bass end of each song differs, and use the EQ to try to even things out. For example, one song might have all of its bass energy bunched up at around 80-90Hz, while another might have an extended deep bass that goes right down to 40Hz or below. By rolling off the sub-bass and peaking up the 80Hz area slightly, it may be possible to bring the bass end back into focus. Similarly, the track with the bunched-up bass could be treated by adding some gentle 40Hz boost, combined with a little cut at around 120Hz. Every equaliser behaves differently, so there are no hard and fast figures – you'll need to experiment.

- At the mid and high end, use a little gentle boost at between 6kHz and 15kHz to add 'air' and presence to a mix, while cutting at between 1kHz and 3kHz to reduce harshness. Boxiness tends to occur between 150Hz and 400Hz. Also, if you need to add some top to a track, try a harmonic enhancer such as an Aphex Exciter (high-end EQ boost will simply increase the hiss). It's important to keep EQ adjustments as subtle as possible, because music that has had a lot of EQ applied to it is more likely to sound processed. Pay particular attention to the timbre of the vocals, and make sure that it stays natural.

- A digital limiter can be used to increase the level of a song that's already peaking close to digital full scale, either as a software plug-in or as part of an external mastering processor. In most cases, the overall level can be increased by up to 6dB or even more before it becomes noticeable that the peaks have been processed in any way. It's always good practice to normalise the loudest track on an album so that it peaks at around -0.5dB and then balance the others to that one, but if you're using a limiter that's also capable of noise-shaped dithering it helps matters if normalising is the last process you use on a track so that you can then use dither to maintain the best possible dynamic range. Normalising, or matching levels in some other way, should always be the last thing you do because EQ, dynamics and enhancement all change levels to some degree.

• If a mix sounds too 'middly', or a little lacking in definition, I find that the SPL Vitalizer is one of the most effective spectral tweaking tools. This device combines the principles of EQ and enhancement in one box, and tends to clean up the mid range at the same time as adding high end and deep bass. However, as with all enhancers, if it's used too much a mix might end up sounding too harsh. You can retain a sense of perspective if you switch the process on and off, and this also applies to EQ and dynamics – regularly check the treated version against the untreated material to make sure that you haven't actually made things worse.

- It's helpful to have a CD player on hand so that you can compare your work with some reference material. Not only does this act as a control for your ears but it will also help you to compensate for any remaining inaccuracies in the monitoring system.

- Compressing an entire mix can give it energy and will also help to even out the performance, but this isn't mandatory. Music needs some 'light and shade' to provide dynamics. Compression will often slightly change the apparent balance of a mix, and so it may need to be used in combination with EQ. Inserting the EQ before the compressor in the signal chain means that any boosted frequencies will be compressed the most, while putting it after the compressor will allow you to equalise the compressed sound without affecting the operation of the device. The most appropriate method will depend on the material being treated, so try both. A split-band compressor or dynamic equaliser will allow you more scope to change the spectral balance of a mix, and will produce the least noticeable side-effects. I find that low thresholds (from -20 to -30dB) and low compression ratios (less than 1.5:1) work best for most material.

- One way to homogenise a mix that either doesn't quite gel or sounds too dry is to add reverb to the entire mix. This has to be done very carefully, however, because excess reverb tends to make things sound 'washy' or cluttered, but I find ambience programs excellent tools with which to give a mix a sense of space and identity without making it sound processed. If the reverb is cluttering up the bass sounds, try rolling off the bass from the reverb send.

If you want to add a stereo-width-enhancing effect to a completed mix, there are two main considerations: the balance of the mix and the mono compatibility of the end result. Most width enhancers increase the level of panned or stereo sounds while slightly suppressing those that occur in the centre of the stereo image. EQ can sometimes be used to compensate for this, but half the battle is just being aware of it. Width enhancement also tends to compromise the sound of a mono mix, so always make sure that it still sounds acceptable with the Mono button depressed. While most serious listening equipment these days is stereo, a lot of televisions and portable radios are still mono, so it's still important that your material is mono compatible.

- Listen to the completed master all the way through, preferably over headphones, because these show up small glitches and noises that loudspeakers may mask. Digital clicks can appear in even the best systems, although the risk of these cropping up can be reduced if you use good-quality digital interconnects that are no longer than necessary.

- If the end product is a CD master, always try to work from a 44.1kHz master tape (or convert the sample rate to 44.1kHz). If you have to work from a 48kHz tape, or from one on which tracks are recorded at different sample rates, use a stand-alone sample-rate converter during the transfer of the material into the computer or use the analogue inputs. Some editing software will allow you convert the sample rate inside the computer, although this makes considerable demands on the processor and the quality is not always as good as that which you'd obtain from a good-quality dedicated unit.

  If you're producing a master for commercial production rather than for making CD-Rs at home, and you don't have the facility to convert sample rates, leave your master at 48kHz and inform the mastering house so that they can handle the conversion for you.

- When transferring digital material into a computer, always make sure that the computer hardware is set to External Digital Sync when recording and Internal Digital Sync when during playback. Also, double check that your recording sample rate matches that of the source – clients will often present you with DAT tapes at the wrong sample rate, or even with different tracks at different sample rates. This happens more often than you might imagine, and if you miss it you may have to start the entire session again.

- If you're using a digital de-noising program, don't expect it to work miracles – even the best systems produce side-effects if you push them too far. The simpler systems are effectively multi-band expanders, on which the threshold of each band is set by first analysing a section of the noise which occurs between tracks. It's therefore best not to try to clean up your original masters before editing, or you'll have no noise samples left. Used carefully, you can get a few decibels of noise reduction before the side-effects become noticeable. These side-effects occur because, as low-level signals open and close the expanders in the various bands, the background noise is modulated in a way that can only be described as 'chirping'. This problem becomes worse the more noise reduction you try to achieve, so it's best to use as little as possible. The technique I use is to reduce the background noise as much as possible while still leaving it high enough to mask any resulting low-level chirping.

• When editing individual tracks – for example, when compiling a version from the best sections of several mixes or recordings – try to make butt joins just before or just after a drum beat so that any discontinuities are masked by the beat. If you have to use a crossfade edit to smooth over a transition, however, try to avoid including a drum beat in the crossfade zone or you may hear a phasing or 'flamming' effect where the two beats overlap. As a rule, crossfades should be as short as possible in order to avoid running into a double-tracking effect during the fade zone, and as little as between 10ms and 30ms is enough to avoid producing a click.

• For important projects, run off an extra backup copy of the final mastered DAT tape or CD-R, and mark these as being either 'production master' or 'clone'. When using CD-R to produce a master that will itself be used for commercial CD production, the disc must be written in Disc-At-Once mode, rather than a track at a time, and the software must support Red Book PQ coding. Check with the production company to confirm that they can work from CD-R as a master, and jot down any special requirements they may have. Be very careful how you handle blank CD-Rs – there are commercial CDs on the market with beautiful fingerprints embodied in the digital data! Also, try and resist the temptation to use cheap blank CD-Rs, as these can produce significantly higher rates of error than good-quality branded discs.

- Stand-alone audio CD recorders often have an automatic shut-off function if gaps in the audio exceed a pre-determined number of seconds (usually between six and 20). This may be a problem if you need to insert large gaps between tracks for any reason, and very quiet passages in classical music are occasionally interpreted as gaps. Also, note that these recorders will continue recording for that same preset number of seconds after the last track, so you'll need to stop recording manually if you don't want a length of silence tacked onto the end of an album.

- When digitally transferring material from a DAT recorder to a CD recorder that can read DAT IDs, it's best to manually edit the DAT IDs first so that they occur around half a second before the start of the track. Placing the first ID two seconds before the start of the first song will remove the risk of missing part of the first note when the track is accessed on a regular CD player.

computer editing

Editing is an important stage of music post
production, and is often carried out at the same
time as mastering. When your stereo masters have
been completed, the chances are that you'll have a
number of differently-mixed versions of each of the
songs required on the finished album, and it's
common practice to create one perfect song from the
best parts of two or more versions. Furthermore, you
may want to change the arrangement of one or more
of your songs – by adding or removing choruses and
shortening solos, for example. All of these operations
require high-precision cut-and-paste editing.

It's also often necessary to remove clicks or other
transient noises, and this isn't always a
straightforward process. Very brief digital clicks can
often be removed by 'drawing in' an approximation of
the correct waveform in the vicinity of the click, while
in other instances the offending section has to be
removed and the remaining parts joined back
together, often with a crossfade to disguise the

discontinuity. This is often the case when the click extends over several cycles of the audio waveform (which may be the case if it were caused by outside electrical interference) or where it has a physical cause, such as a lip smack, a page turn or a bow tapping against a cello. Some software packages are equipped with special click-removing tools which may be more effective at achieving this than doing the job manually, although manual redrawing can be quite effective after a little practice. This job is a lot easier if the software is capable of automatically smoothing redrawn sections, and there is a smaller chance of leaving any audible evidence of the edit.

the editing procedure

When the mixes that you intend to use on the album have been loaded into the computer (ideally by digital transfer from a DAT recorder, or something similar), any complete songs will then need to be topped and tailed. It's at the this stage that unwanted count-ins are removed. The end of the track will often need to be faded out, either with a conventionally long fade-out or perhaps with the very end of the last decaying note faded to silence, providing a smooth, clean ending. If no further editing is required, the topped and tailed songs must then be placed in the correct running order with suitable gaps between them, and the levels must be examined (and adjusted if necessary) so that all of the tracks sit together comfortably. It may also prove necessary to equalise songs which have been mixed at different times in order to make the album sound more homogeneous, and in extreme cases it may be desirable to add a little artificial ambience to an otherwise completed mix so that all of the songs sound as though they were recorded in the same acoustic environment. These processes were touched upon in earlier chapters, and they may be carried out with either hardware or software equalisers and limiters. However, if you intend to tackle only the editing, leaving the mastering to a professional, it's probably best not to apply any overall EQ or any form of dynamic processing, as the professionals will almost certainly have better tools and more experience.

On the other hand, if you're planning on taking the project to the point at which it's ready for production then you'll need to be able to equalise, compress and limit your material, and this should ideally be carried out within the digital domain. You'll also need editing software that allows you to undertake precise cut-and-paste editing, as well as normalising, fading and gain adjustment.

tools of the trade

Most mastering systems are now computer based, and there are viable options available for both Mac and PC users. A soundcard or interface with digital I/O is essential for any serious work, but it's always useful to have high-quality analogue input converters in order to handle jobs that come in on analogue tape or that need to be processed with an analogue equaliser. It all depends on whether the facility is for your own personal use or whether you intend to undertake some commercial work. For commercial work, your A-to-D (Analogue-to-Digital) converters should ideally be capable of working at 24-bit resolution, so that analogue tape recordings can be transferred into your system at maximum resolution. In this way, when the final file is reduced to 16-bit resolution for CD mastering, noise-shaped dithering can be used to retain as much as possible of the original dynamic range. Sample-rate conversion is a process that will also necessary on those occasions when clients turn up with 48kHz masters recorded with domestic digital recorders, because the edited master should always be at 44.1kHz if it's destined for CD production. If the facility is for your own use, and you work exclusively at a sampling rate of 44.1kHz, it's possible to get by without having to use sample-rate conversion. (At the moment I don't feel that

96kHz mastering is relevant, although everybody seems to be including it in their software and hardware in order to make it more marketable.)

hardware signal processing

It's often possible to equalise and process levels and dynamics within the computer by using software plug-ins, but you will sometimes need to use a hardware mastering processor. The top-of-the-range models of these devices combine parametric EQ with functions such as de-essing, dynamic EQ, multiband compression, multiband limiting, multiband expansion and tube simulation. They also usually provide the user with control over stereo width and left/right balance.

With a hardware processor it's possible to either process the material while it's being recording to a hard drive or play back the edited material on the processor itself, recording the result to DAT or some other suitable storage medium. Processing while recording provides the advantage that it's not necessary to send the file back out to a DAT machine before a CD can be made, but also it means that any subsequent fine-tuning will have to be done in software. Processing the finished file, on the other hand, means that settings can be created to suit each track individually, and you can check how they sound together before sending the file out to a DAT machine.

On a conventional album, there should be enough time during the gaps between the tracks to change presets on the mastering processor, but you'll probably have to do this by hand because none of the editors that I've come across allow the user to output MIDI Program Change messages between tracks in a playlist, which I feel is a very obvious function. If your CD burner is a computer peripheral rather than a stand-alone unit, the quickest way to process is to do it as you record to the hard disk. However, it's also possible to process the audio as it's played back to DAT, and then to load the DAT material back onto the hard drive so that you can compile the final playlist. As long as you work in the digital domain, there should be no appreciable degradation in quality.

Digital mastering processors have the advantage that they offer simultaneous access to all of the commonly-used mastering processes without imposing too much of a burden on your computer. Because they don't rely on using a computer's CPU, they may also be able to provide a higher quality of processing than a software-based system.

audio storage

Once you've chosen a suitable computer and interface, you'll need to fit a separate drive for your audio work. A completed album seldom takes up more than 750Mb (megabytes), but you will need to allow space to store alternative takes, temporary files and, in some cases, image files of the completed tracks or album. Almost any modern AV drive should be fast enough for stereo editing, whether SCSI or IDE, but the manufacturers of your editing software may also recommend specific models of drives, in which case it's best to choose one from their approved list. Given that large drives are relatively cheap, it's a good idea to use a separate drive of 10Gb (gigabytes) or larger for your audio work.

Most people choose a computer and then look for software to run on it, but it's a more sensible approach to find a piece of software that fits your requirements and then find a suitable computer on which to run it. Although there are a number of software packages on the market that are capable of wave editing, few have the tools needed to edit between sections of a song precisely. It helps to be able to see the waveform on either side of an edit, but it's more important to be able to loop around the edit point while nudging the start and end points in (preferably user-definable) increments so that you can time this accurately. Pop music isn't particularly difficult, because an edit on a drum beat will be easily visible in the waveform display, but in classical music the visual clues may be almost non-existent, and it's here that the ability to 'fine-nudge' proves absolutely vital. If you're new to using editing software, I'd recommend that you talk to a few other users, or at least visit a few special-interest web sites to see what existing users have to say about the software they're using. In this way, you may also be able to pick up important information concerning hardware and software incompatibility problems.

regions

The first thing to do when starting any project is to divide the audio file up into regions, and invariably there will be some kind of overview waveform that will illustrate how the whole file looks. Creating regions doesn't actually change the original file, but it does make it possible to move and copy regions as though they were separate items. In all of the packages which I've tried, it's possible to zoom in on the main waveform window so that you can position the cursor more precisely before defining the start and end points of the region. The ability to perform 'audio scrubbing' is also very important, as it's often possible to identify an edit point by ear when the shape of the waveform provides insufficient clues. The regions you define will include complete songs, where no further editing is needed, and sections of songs where you're creating a new arrangement, either by editing one block of material or by combining sections from different takes.

Another effective way of defining edit points is to mark the starts and ends of regions 'on the fly'. This usually involves playing the audio through in real time and then hitting a key on the computer keyboard to mark the edit point. As long as you have a reasonable sense of rhythm, it should be possible to get very close to the perfect edit point using this method, especially if the music has a clearly-defined beat.

After being defined, these regions are generally assembled in a playlist, after which you can audition the transition between one region and the next. If you're compiling a song from a number of different sections, it's at this point – at the transition between sections – that you need to make fine adjustments to the start and end times of a region. It's often not enough just to get the timing right, as there may still be a small click at the edit point, especially if the edit isn't masked by a drum beat, and so a crossfade must be made between these regions. A crossfade of 10-20ms is generally enough to avoid clicks, while still producing a seamless edit.

It's also a good idea to check out how the software handles things when you remove a short section from the middle of a file and join up the two severed ends. Some programs can do this in a non-destructive way (ie the file is only changed permanently when the material is actively saved), but some others actually erase the selected data from disk and then move back the rest of the material to close the gap. When working with an album-length file, this can mean a long delay while the file is rewritten.

You can generally achieve the same thing in a non-destructive way, however, if you create new regions on either side of the section you want to remove. However, this can be tedious with albums containing spoken-word material or similar, where there may be many gaps to close up and *umm*s to lose.

Virtually all editing software allows you to perform at least one level of undo, but some allow only one level, so check each edit once you've made it before moving on. This style of editing has a huge advantage over tape splicing, where the undo process involves sticky tape and razor blades! Most modern editing software also offers VST plug-in support, which makes it possible to add software tools for equalisation, limiting, compression and so on as and when you need them.

editing with a sequencer

If you usually mix songs in such a way that they don't need much further editing, the audio capabilities of most audio-plus-MIDI sequencers are easily capable of stringing an album together, and because most of these devices use VST plug-ins it's also possible to perform a reasonable amount of signal processing. All of the major packages (such as Cubase VST and Logic Audio) allow you to change the level of a section of audio as well as apply fade-ins and fade-outs, and changes in gain or fades can usually be drawn in as an envelope. However, unlike dedicated audio editors, these packages don't offer convenient tools for the auditioning and adjusting of edits between regions.

a typical editing session

The first step in any album editing project is to load all of the audio material onto the hard drive of the computer. Unless you're using an analogue source, or you intend to access material via an analogue processor, it's best to transfer material in the digital domain in order to avoid the loss in quality that invariably occurs when a signal makes an unnecessary trip via the A-to-D converters of a soundcard or audio interface. To obtain the highest-quality recording, it's best to work at bit depths in excess of 16 bit and then dither down to 16 bits at the final stage of processing, but in reality most work arrives in a 16-bit format already, as it appears on DAT and CD-R.

On some software packages it doesn't matter if you record your songs as separate audio files or as one long single file, although some packages require everything to be part of the same file in order to play back a complete album to DAT in real time. However, I prefer to create and edit regions in the editing software and then use a CD-burning program to import regions that have been created in the editor. In this way, it's possible to import regions from different sound files, if necessary.

Whichever method you end up adopting, if you're using a digital source you should double check that your software is set to External Digital Sync before recording. If you forget to switch, you'll end up with a file full of ticks, clicks and glitches, and you'll have to start the whole project all over again.

more about regions

The terminology involved varies between one piece of software to another, but the first stage in editing invariably involves dividing the audio file up into regions. This is akin to chopping up an analogue tape into sections, discarding any unnecessary material, and then splicing the pieces together. The main difference is that computer editing is largely non-destructive, and so, even though the user interface may tell you that you've created lots of little regions, the source audio file hasn't actually been changed. It's also possible to use the same region more than once, which is impossible with analogue tape unless it's physically copied first.

The overview waveform of the entire file serves as a useful navigation aid because, at the very least, it will give you a good idea of where one songs stops and the next one starts. Once you're in the right area, you can play the file until the start of the song and then zoom in on the waveform display to find the exact point of the start of the wanted audio.

Sometimes the first sound of a song isn't actually the point at which the song should start – there may be squeaking guitar strings, for example, or the rattle of a snare drum, or even a count-in that you'd prefer not to have. In situations like these an editor with an 'audio scrub' function comes in very useful, as you can move back and forth across any section of audio at any speed and compare what you can see on the screen with what you're hearing. It generally isn't necessary to erase the unwanted material, but you should make sure that the start point of the region comes after it.

It's also worth pointing out that a vocal intro may be preceded by a breath, and it's not always a good idea to take this out. In editing there are just as many artistic decisions as there are technical ones, so let your ears decide what works best. Sometimes it's okay to leave a breath sound in place, but it may be a good idea to drop the level by a few decibels.

Defining the ends of songs isn't quite as easy, because most songs have a little reverb at the end of the last note, which may itself sustain and decay over quite a long period. It's usually possible to use the vertical (amplitude) zoom facility on an editor to make it clear where the meaningful audio stops, although it's just as effective to turn up the monitoring gain and use the audio scrub tool. Most recordings contain a little background noise, so to keep things tidy I usually finish with a short fade-out, starting just before the audio fades to nothingness and extending for a second or so. This ensures that the song fades to complete silence.

To add a gradual fade-out to a song, you'll need to make the fade time around 25 or 30 seconds long if you don't want it to sound rushed. It's best to silence any material that remains after the fade, but before you do this make sure that the fade sounds okay while you still have the chance to undo it. Some packages offer different fade curves, so try out all of the alternatives to find the one which sounds the most natural. I prefer to perform fades after normalising or equalising, but I have to admit that, on most pop material, there's no subjective difference if they're performed beforehand.

levels

As long as there's no editing that needs to be done within the songs themselves, the next task – after identifying the regions that define the individual songs on the album – is to ensure that each track has a consistent sound and level. Listen to the rhythm track and the vocal levels to try and gain a feel for the relative balance of the songs, and if you're still not sure whether or not something is too loud then try listening from the next room with the door open. This seems to focus the mind on how the music balances, rather than on any other issues. When doing this, however, it's important to use your ears, and not the level meters.

If not all of the songs are recorded at a high enough level, you may need to normalise low-level songs before you continue. The process of normalising simply increases the level of gain, so that the loudest peak in the song is at 0dB DFS (Digital Full Scale). After normalising, the playback gain for the track can be turned down until it sits comfortably with the rest of the album (there's usually a gain control for individual regions in editing programs or on a CD burner's playlist).

If the songs were recorded or mixed at different times, you may well have to deal with tonal differences. A good way of working here is to find the best-sounding song (tonally, not necessarily musically) on the album and then try and EQ the other tracks so that they sound similar. As always, EQ boost should be used sparingly. Cut can be used a little more aggressively, but listen carefully for any hint of the sound becoming unnatural or nasal. Every EQ situation is different, but if you have a parametric plug-in you could try a little 15kHz boost within a three-octave bandwidth, which will add sheen and detail without imparting any harshness. Presence can be added by gently boosting at 4-6kHz, bass sounds can be given added punchiness at 80-90Hz using a one- to two-octave bandwidth setting, and drums and instruments which sound too boxy can be tamed by cutting at around 150Hz using a one-octave width setting. Deep bass can be adjusted with the addition of cut or boost at around 40-50Hz, and vocals which sound too thick can sometimes be improved by cutting at around 200-250Hz. Always approach EQ very carefully, and make good use of your Bypass button to make sure that you haven't applied too much. A good equaliser should allow you to make the necessary changes with only a decibel or two of cut and boost.

Another useful mastering trick is to apply overall compression, but it's generally best to stick to very low ratios (ie less than 1.5:1) and low thresholds. Even a ratio of as little as 1.1:1 can make a track sound much bigger and much more even. Using auto attack and release can also help a great deal, especially with material that is constantly changing in dynamics, and a multiband compressor is likely to produce more satisfactory results than a basic full-band unit. If the threshold is set at around -30dB or thereabouts, gentle compression will be applied to all but the quietest sections of the mix.

A good separate limiter can also be used to increase the level of a mix by limiting the top 3dB or 4dB of the signal. This means that the overall level can then be increased by the same amount before clipping occurs, and if this is done before reducing the signal to 16 bits then more low-level resolution will be retained. A number of software mastering limiter plug-ins perform this task exceptionally well, although a multiband limiter will allow more gain reduction to be applied before any side-effects become evident.

compiling from regions

The fun starts when you have to edit songs together from various sections. Selecting the individual regions that make up a song can be done by marking start and end points on the fly and then adjusting the material in the playlist until the timing is right. With pop music, it's generally best if the edit points coincide with the start of a drum beat, as this provides a good visual landmark and also helps to hide any discontinuities that might arise when the two sections come from two different mixes. (Figure 4.1 illustrates this simple edit.) However, you'll eventually come across an edit where there's a

Figure 4.1: A basic edit

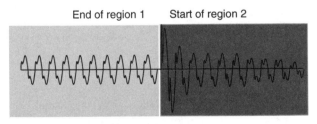

If the edit is made immediately before a drum beat, any glitch caused by less-than-perfect timing is likely to be hidden

vocal running over the edit point, and the singer doesn't use exactly the same timing in both takes. In this case, if the edit is done on the beat the timing of the backing track will be fine but the vocal will have a noticeable jump in the middle of a word. The best way to get around this is probably to first set the initial edit points on the beat and then go into the playlist and nudge the edit backwards or forwards in time in small increments (both the end of the first region and the start of the second) until the edit has been moved to a point so that it falls between words. Of course, it may now be the case that there is no drumbeat to hide the edit, but it may help if you can line up the edit with a hi-hat beat or some other percussive event. If all else fails, try a short crossfade. While crossfades aren't foolproof, they will solve most problems if used carefully.

tricky edits

When editing classical music, or some other style of music with no obvious rhythmic edit points that act as landmarks in the waveform display, the best way to work is to mark up the regions on the fly, place the regions in order within the software's playlist, and then loop around each edit point and nudge the end of one region or the start of the next until the timing is right. Only then should you worry about trying to disguise the edit.

As with the previous example involving two slightly different vocal performances, you may need to nudge the whole edit backwards or forwards in time until you find a point that produces a smooth join, although you may need to perform a short crossfade to smoothe things over properly. When moving edit points like this, it's a good idea to record a few more seconds of audio than you need at either end of each section.

If the edit doesn't coincide with a strong beat, you may find that there's an audible glitch at the edit point, and there is a myth that making the edit at waveform zero crossing points will guarantee no glitching – it won't. You'll only avoid a glitch if the waveform on one side of the edit flows smoothly into the waveform at the other side, and Figure 4.2 shows that, even if the waveforms on either side of the edit are identical, there are two possible scenarios, one which will cause a glitch and one which won't. In the first example, the waveforms on either side of the edit are in phase, so the transition will be smooth; in the second, however, they are out of phase, resulting in a discontinuity at the edit point, causing a click.

crossfade edits

The usual way of solving an awkward edit is to use a crossfade between the two regions, but again these aren't foolproof. A crossfade involves fading one region out after the edit point while at the same time fading in the second region before the edit point (which is itself another reason for recording a few seconds more material at both ends of each section), but the problem with crossfades is that they are just fades that occur between two sounds, and so both sounds are audible in changing proportions for the duration of the crossfade, with the balance being equal in the middle of the crossfade. Unless the sounds are absolutely identical, and in phase, this may cause a double tracking or chorus-like effect, which is one reason to keep crossfades as short as possible. Furthermore, if there is a drastic phase shift between the sounds on either side of the crossfade, there may be a noticeable dip in level in the middle of the crossfade, as shown in Figure 4.3. Applying a crossfade is less likely to cause level changes if you can arrange things so that your edit points occur at zero crossing points, and the waveforms on either side of the edit are in phase.

Try and avoid long crossfades over percussive beats, which can produce a 'flamming' effect if the timing of the two beats isn't exactly right. As a rule, a crossfade of 20ms or so is long enough to prevent clicks, although a longer one may be required to smoothe out an awkward transition.

Figure 4.2: Zero crossing points

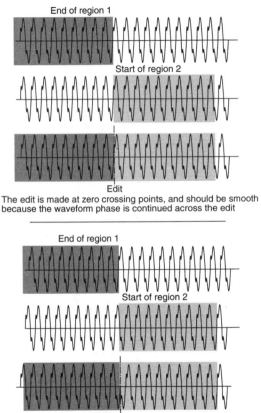

The edit is made at zero crossing points, and should be smooth because the waveform phase is continued across the edit

The edit is made at zero crossing points, but there will be a glitch because the waveform phase is not continued across the edit

Figure 4.3: Crossfade edits

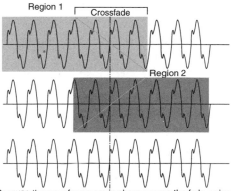

Because the waveforms are in phase across the fade region, there is no amplitude change and the edit is smooth

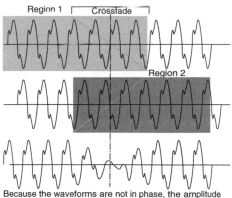

Because the waveforms are not in phase, the amplitude changes across the fade region

In those situations where the material on either side of the crossfade is well matched (for example, if the regions are from two takes of the same song and mixed similarly), it's important to keep the fades as short as possible while still making the edit smooth. If the material is completely different on both sides of an edit (two different pieces of music, for example, or a decaying last note followed by a burst of spontaneous applause), you can use any length of crossfade necessary; because the waveforms aren't correlated in any way there won't be any phase cancellation.

clicks and glitches

Editing occasionally involves fixing problems, as well as making artistic decisions, and few problems are as irritating as clicks. There are currently some very sophisticated software packages available for the practise of identifying and removing clicks, and if you have access to a program that can do this then I'd suggest that you try it, to see if it can perform the necessary invisible mends. As a rule, the more expensive commercial systems are the best at achieving this, although there are some VST plug-ins available that are also reasonably effective. Also, it's generally possible to remove clicks manually if they are readily identifiable and relatively infrequent.

If you don't have specialised click-removing tools, this can often be done manually with the use of simple edits and crossfades. Brief, easily-identifiable clicks are best tackled by drawing them out with the editor's pencil tool, but make sure that the smoothing tool is switched on first, if available, as it will help to make sure that your newly-drawn section doesn't cause a click of its own.

In those situations where the glitch covers a longer period of time, and drawing is not a suitable way to get rid of it, another useful technique is to create two regions, where one stops a few cycles before the click and the next starts a few cycles later. Line up the edit points so that they occur on zero crossings and are in phase and then use a short crossfade to smoothe the join. If you're lucky, the tiny portion of audio you've lost in getting rid of the click won't throw out the timing too much. In this situation, it's important not to edit too close to the click you're trying to remove, or the click will be allowed to creep back in when you implement the crossfade. The same is also true if the crossfade is too long, as can be seen from Figure 4.4a, and if you're planning to use a crossfade of 10ms you'll need to leave at least 5ms of material on both sides of the click to avoid this. Figure 4.4b shows a section of waveform complete with several problem areas that would cause clicks, although most of these could be

Figure 4.4a: Removing clicks

If the regions on either side of the click are crossfaded fairly quickly, the click will be removed and a smooth edit is possible, as long as the phase of the waveforms on either side of the edit match well enough not to cause a dip in level

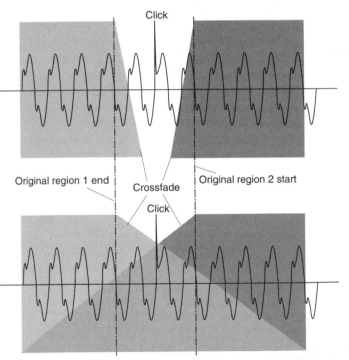

If the crossfade region is extended too far in the hope of obtaining a smoother edit, because the section of the waveform which includes the click is included within the crossfade it will become audible again

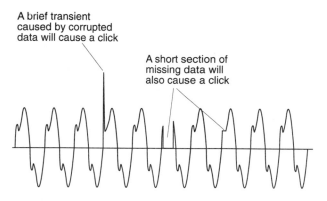

A brief transient
caused by corrupted
data will cause a click

A short section of
missing data will
also cause a click

Figure 4.4b: Problems with clicks

cured by redrawing and smoothing the affected area.
(Note that not all clicks are caused by obvious spikes in
the waveform.)

Unfortunately, not all clicks are this straightforward;
some are caused by short bursts of interference, which
may extend for several cycles. Furthermore, a click
which has occurred prior to the mixing of a track may
also have reverb added to it! Close scrutiny of the
waveform often fails to reveal anything amiss, other
than a very low level of high-frequency 'fuzz'
superimposed on the waveform. This type of problem
is generally too complex to be cured by drawing in a
cycle or two of waveform, so performing an edit on

either side of the click and crossfading may be the most effective option. Whether the timing of the song is affected or not will depend on the length of the interference and on the timing of the music.

As a last resort, you may be able to replace a damaged or corrupted section of audio with a short section copied from elsewhere. For example, if you find a click or a patch of interference in the middle of a sustained note you may be able to plug the gap by copying and pasting a few cycles from immediately before or immediately after the affected section. Alternatively, you may be able to find an identical bar elsewhere in the song which you can splice in. This, however, requires a great deal of skill and patience because, if the ends of the new section of waveform don't line up exactly with the existing material, this will also produce a click. You will also need to look carefully at the pattern of the waveform and pick a sequence of cycles that appears to match the damaged section fairly closely, and most real-world audio is considerably more complex than a continuous sine wave. Editing is generally more successful if the editing package has an automatic smoothing option which can be used for these kinds of edits. It may be possible to smoothe out minor discontinuities between edits manually, by using the drawing tool, but it's often very difficult to produce a seamless edit in this way unless your system has a smoothing facility. Sometimes it's easier to edit in a longer section, such as an entire musical phrase or even a verse (as long as a suitable section exists elsewhere in the song), as a separate playlist region.

equalisation

Digital equaliser plug-ins can be extremely useful when editing, but as always there are potential problem involved. Firstly, if you intend to apply a significant amount of equalising, make sure that you have enough audio headroom available, especially if you're using boosts. If necessary, you should reduce the level of the original file before working on it (although most of the better-quality equaliser packages include a gain control).

A less obvious problem is that most equalisers introduce a degree of phase shift, and so if you were to select a section of audio and then equalise just that section, for example, you'd probably end up with an audible glitch at the start and the end of the treated section. This is a direct result of the EQ phase shift – the equalised and unequalised sections are now slightly displaced in time, in effect, and so the waveforms no longer join smoothly. The only reliable way to use EQ in most systems is either to EQ the entire song or break it up into regions and EQ only specific regions. In this way, short crossfades can be used to ensure that the region transitions are free from clicks. Unfortunately, this also means that you're unlikely to get away with (for example) selecting a short section of audio containing a vocal pop and then applying heavy bass cut just to that section. However, it's still worth trying this approach, as long as you have the ability to undo it afterwards, because some designs of digital EQ cause more phase-shift problems that others. An editor with a smoothing function may also be more forgiving when regions are EQ'd within a file.

putting it all together

After working on the basic songs, you should have a number of regions representing finished songs, complete with any destructive processing (such as level increases, compression, EQ and limiting) already done. If you also have access to de-noising software, you should use the process as gently as possible, because overuse often introduces unpleasant side-effects in low-level passages or fade-outs.

In those instances where songs are edited together from two or more regions, these will also be assembled in the playlist with a gap between the regions set to zero and suitable crossfades used where necessary. However, if you intend to export the regions to a CD-burning program, it may be best to save any heavily-edited songs as new sound files. In most packages, the easiest way of doing this is to create a playlist for each edited song and then use the 'Save Playlist As New Soundfile' option to create a new, single file for the song. This new file can then be imported into your CD-burning program.

Once you have created a playlist with all of the songs in the correct running order, you can decrease the levels of any songs that are too loud and set artistically-suitable gap lengths between the tracks. (When defining gap lengths, I usually have two or three seconds between songs and then fine tune this until it feels right.) You may not need a particularly long gap after songs with slow fade-outs, but if there's a noticeable change in mood or tempo between songs you may feel that a longer gap is more suitable. There's no sure-fire method of calculating the right length of gap, just as there is no method of calculating the correct relative levels for different tracks on an album – it just has to feel right.

The next step will depend on whether you're going to make a master DAT or whether you want to burn a CD.

Personally, I like to create new audio files for any tracks that comprise two or more regions if I'm burning the material directly onto a CD, but this is unnecessary if you're planning to play the album from your editor so that you can record it back onto DAT.

Before playing a file back to DAT you should make sure the editor hardware is set back to Internal Sync, and afterwards you may need to adjust the DAT start IDs. If you let the Auto mode do its thing then each ID will be slightly late, because an ID can't be written until the machine detects some audio material. Because of this, you may wish to erase the DAT IDs and write in new ones which occur a fraction of a second earlier. You should also leave a gap of at least two seconds between the first ID and the start of the music, especially if you're going to copy the DAT onto a CD-R with a stand-alone recorder, because these sometimes take a second or two to pick up from a standing start.

burning a CD

If you're burning material onto a CD which you intend to use as a production master, it's important to use software that's Red Book compliant. Figure 4.5 shows the playlist from a commercial CD-burning software package, indicating where the levels of individual

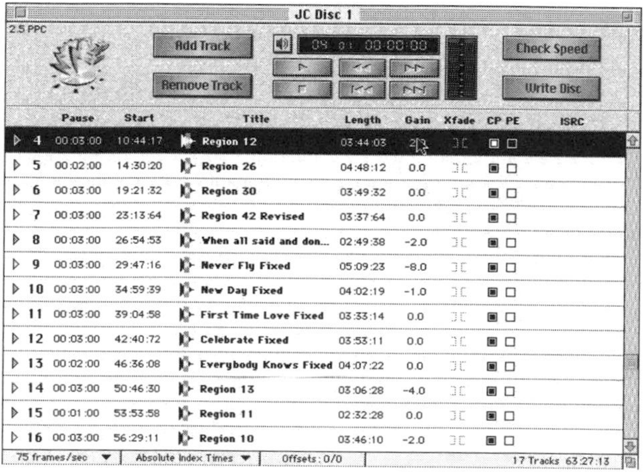

Figure 4.5: CD burning playlist

regions can be increased by up to 6dB or attenuated as much as necessary. As with all digital software, if the level increases to the point at which clipping occurs, this results in some very nasty crunches and bangs, so it's a good idea to normalise each track separately before importing it and then use the gain controls in the CD burner's playlist to reduce the levels of those tracks that need to be quieter. In this case a perfect balance can be achieved without running the risk of clipping.

If a good CD-burning package is used, it will also be

possible to encode snatches of text in the CD's subcode, such as the album details and IRSC codes for the individual tracks (codes that uniquely identify each track, for the purposes of copyright tracking). It's also possible to toggle the Copy Prohibit flag on each individual track, as well as to select whether or not tracks should be played back with de-emphasis. As most modern DAT recorders don't record with pre-emphasis, this box will normally be left unchecked. All parts of the playlist may be auditioned, just to confirm that everything is OK before going for the burn. After this, it's time to slip in that CD-R and make your production master.

On the subject of burning CD-Rs, I generally burn mine at four times the normal speed because most blank discs are optimised for this speed. If your computer is a little on the slow side, it often proves helpful to create a disc image of the entire album before starting (which can take up to 640Mb of hard disk space). I can't emphasise too strongly the false economy of using cheap, unbranded CD-R blanks – some of them have astoundingly high error rates, and you can't be really sure about their life expectancy.

It's vitally important that any CD-R blanks which you're going to use as production masters are scrupulously clean, so don't open the packet until you're ready to use the disc, and always hold it by its edges. Make sure that there's no dust on the recording surface, and if you need to remove any dust particles then a quick squirt from a can of compressed air, purchased from a local camera shop, will do as good as job as anything. Under no circumstances should you touch the recording surface with your fingers, as this will play havoc with the error rate.

CDs intended for use as production masters should always be recorded in one pass (Disc-At-Once mode), because pausing the recording process introduces errors between tracks with which some duplication plants can't cope.

that little red book

Audio CDs, as I have already said, are manufactured to Red Book standard. But what does 'Red Book' and 'PQ encoding' actually mean? These terms relate to an attempt to create a standard that will allow any audio CD to work on any player. An audio CD has a data capacity of around 650Mb, and a standard disc can hold up to 74 minutes of audio (although discs that can hold more material are now available). Unlike a vinyl record or tape, where only continuous audio is recorded, audio CDs break up the data into smaller sectors, and each sector can hold up to 2,352 bytes of data. On an audio disc, most of this data carries audio material, while a CD-ROM – which has a similar structure – will use the space to store digital data, which is why the same blank discs can be used to record either audio or data. However, an audio CD also contains non-audio data, relating to lengths and numbers of tracks, total playing times, remaining time and so on.

An audio CD is comprised of three distinct areas: Lead In, Programme and Lead Out. The Lead In occurs at the start of the disc (which on a CD is in the centre), and it's here that the table of contents is located, which the CD player can refer to in order to find out how may tracks are on the CD, their location, the length of the material on the disc, and so on. After this comes the Programme area, where the audio material itself is stored. The Lead Out section occurs at the end of the Programme section, and signifies the end of the disc. The way in which data is recorded on the disc is governed by the Red Book standard, so a CD-R which is intended for use as a production master must also be compiled to Red Book specifications. The Red Book standard stipulates the 16-bit, 44.1kHz stereo file format, and specifies the way in which this is encoded. The standard also sets out the data structure in order to allow error correction to work, provides space for flags (such as Copy Prohibit and Emphasis flags), and provides space for non-audio data, such as track ISRC codes (which are used to label each track with a serial number) and MCNs (Media Catalogue Numbers), which correspond to the bar code on the packaging. And also, of course, all that clever PQ stuff.

Each sector on an audio CD has 98 bytes reserved for sub-channel control data, although only the first few of these are used to hold data concerning pause and track start data. The rest were included to allow the format to be expanded at a future date, but they are rarely used. The 'P' sub-channel information indicates the location of the start and end of the music on each track, while the 'Q' sub-channel contains information relating to absolute and relative time, ISRC codes (if used), Media Catalogue Numbers (if used) and indexes. Indexes are locator markers within tracks, although few commercial CD players can read them. It's possible for material to be recorded in the pauses between tracks, so if you make a live recording and want the applause to carry through from one track to another, some of this could be located in the pause area. (The pauses between tracks can be set to any size.)

In the Lead In area of the CD, the 'Q' subchannel contains the table of contents, which allows the CD player to know how much material is on the disk, the exact number of tracks that are present and the time at which each begins. Without the table of contents, the CD player wouldn't be able to find the start of each track. A Red Book CD can contain up to 99 separate audio tracks, each with a minimum length of four seconds, and each track can contain up to 99 index points.

chapter 5

monitoring

The importance of accurate monitoring has already been stated, but this chapter concentrates on setting up a monitoring system that's suitable for mastering in the home studio, paying particular attention to problems commonly encountered and their solutions. Without an accurate monitoring system, it's impossible to hear exactly what's going onto a production master tape.

monitoring criteria

The simple aim of a monitoring system in a studio or a mastering suite is to provide an accurate reference by which work can be confidently judged. Unfortunately, there is no such thing as a standard monitor loudspeaker, and even if there were it would still sound different in different acoustic environments and different positions. Because of this, a degree of pragmatism is necessary in order to allow mixes to be created or modified so that they sound acceptable on most domestic audio systems.

A monitor speaker must be as tonally accurate as possible, and should be capable of reproducing the entire audio spectrum with the minimum of distortion or coloration at each frequency. Smaller monitoring systems won't be able to reproduce frequencies as low as full-range systems, of course, but for serious mastering work a reasonable degree of bass extension is necessary, otherwise there's no way of knowing what the bass end really sounds like. Monitors that roll off at around 45-50Hz are ideal in the home studio, as any greater bass extension is likely to interact with the acoustics of the room, making it even more difficult to hear how the bass end is behaving.

off-axis performance

While some speakers are reasonably accurate if you're standing directly in front of them, it's also important that they behave well off axis. Why should this be so? Sound bounces off hard surfaces, and what we hear when we listen to a pair of loudspeakers in a typical room is a combination of the direct (on-axis) sound, along with some off-axis sound that has reflected from the walls. If the off-axis sound is inaccurate in any way, the proportion of what we hear that is due to reflected sound will also be inaccurate. Indeed, it's largely because of the differences in off-axis performance that two loudspeakers with similar specifications can sound very different in the same room. With a good pair of monitors, it should be possible to move from one side of the room to the other and hear a nominally constant tonal balance. The high frequencies will drop away if you move a long way off axis, but this should happen smoothly and unobtrusively.

the room's influence

Virtually all large-scale professional monitoring systems are designed to take into account the acoustic environment in which they are likely to be used; indeed, if a studio is being built from scratch, the chances are that the monitoring system and the room will be designed together. Full-range monitors are generally built into the walls, and are known as soffit-mounted monitors, although most near-field and mid-sized monitors are designed to be used on stands positioned a little way behind the mixing console.

A professional studio designer will probably design a room to have a reverb time that is reasonably short, and nominally equal at all audio frequencies. The acoustic properties of domestic rooms can vary a lot, but a room complete with fitted carpets, soft furnishings and curtains is usually damped well enough to carry out mixing or mastering over smaller monitors. You can't expect to generate very deep bass in a small room because the dimensions are incapable of supporting the long wavelengths involved, which is why large monitors capable of generating very low frequencies aren't recommended.

A good two-way mid-field monitor with a soft domed tweeter is usually the best to use when mastering, and these are well worth considering now that active versions of some small monitors are becoming more affordable, as they eliminate all of the guesswork involved in buying a power amplifier. Active speakers also seem to produce better control over the low-frequency end of the audio spectrum.

positioning monitors

The placement of monitor loudspeakers within a room will affect their performance to a significant degree, because of the way in which low frequencies behave. At mid and high frequencies the sound radiates from the loudspeaker in the form of a cone, but as the frequency reduces in wavelength the radiation pattern widens until, at very low frequencies, the speakers are virtually omnidirectional, with almost as much energy being directed backwards as forwards. This low-frequency

Figure 5.1: A typical monitoring arrangement

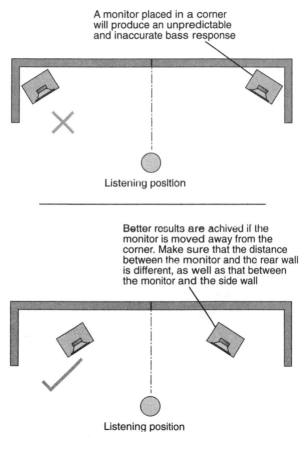

A monitor placed in a corner
will produce an unpredictable
and inaccurate bass response

Listening position

Better results are achived if the
monitor is moved away from the
corner. Make sure that the distance
between the monitor and the rear wall
is different, as well as that between
the monitor and the side wall

Listening position

energy reflects from solid walls but passes through less substantial structures. Any solid wall adjacent to and behind the speakers will bounce energy back into the room, and the perceived bass level within the room will be louder. Sadly, this 'free' bass boost will occur at different frequencies depending on the exact distances between the speakers, the floor, the walls and the ceiling, and if the speakers are too close to the boundaries of the room the bass performance can become very erratic.

The distances between the speaker and the nearer surfaces should be different and as random as possible to prevent all of the reflections combining at the same frequency and to ensure the smoothest and most accurate bass response. For example, it would be a bad idea to place a speaker in a corner, exactly halfway between the floor and the ceiling, as this would produce a bass response interspersed with large peaks and troughs, with the result that some bass notes would sound much louder than others. If the distances from the speaker to the nearest two walls, the floor and the ceiling are all different, and the reflections combine in a more random – and hence more benign – manner.

It's wise to consult the recommendations which manufacturers include with their monitors, but as a rule they should be mounted at least a foot from the wall behind the mixing console and at least 18 inches from the side walls. (Figure 5.1 shows how monitors should and shouldn't be positioned.) In rectangular rooms, the speakers should be set up along the longest wall to ensure the most accurate reproduction, but don't worry too much if this isn't possible.

Some people place speakers on the meter bridge of the mixing console – and some are actually designed to work in this position – but this setup is less than ideal for mastering. Most speakers will sound more accurate if they're positioned on stands a little way behind the console, and it's important that the whole setup is symmetrical. Mounting the speakers behind the mixing console reduces the amount of sound reflected from the console's surface that reaches the listener, which would otherwise combine with the direct sound and cause comb filtering, compromising the accuracy of the sound. Therefore, the less there is the better.

Most monitors are built to be mounted vertically, so that the tweeter is above the bass unit, rather than set on their side, as this provides the widest accurate listening area. This isn't quite as important on speakers on which the bass units and tweeters are close together, but if possible the speakers should be positioned the way in which they were intended.

It's important to position the speakers so that the tweeters are pointed towards the head of the listener, as this will serve to ensure that the listener is on axis with the monitor. However, to widen this 'sweet spot' a little, it may be a better arrangement to position the tweeters so that sound intersects just behind the engineer's head. If this arrangement is impractical, it's acceptable to stand the speakers upside down, with the tweeter at head height, or to angle the speakers with wedges.

Monitor stands should be solid, with no tendency to vibrate, and the monitor itself should be mounted on soft rubber pads, or even small lumps of Blu-Tac, which will both stop them slipping and intercept the cabinet vibrations before they reach the floor. Metal stands can be filled with sand to reduce resonance.

amplifier power

Conventional wisdom used to suggest that using a small power amplifier was the best way of stopping speakers from overloading, but in recent years the reverse has been proven to be true. Most speakers will be able to withstand short periods of overloading, as long as the input signal isn't distorted or clipped too much. However, an underpowered amplifier can easily be driven into clipping, which will cause a harmonically-rich, clipped waveform to be fed into the tweeters. Apart from sounding disgusting, this can easily overheat the tweeter's voice coil, causing it to burn out.

It's safest to buy the largest amplifier recommended for your speakers, and ideally it should have clip indicators to warn you if clipping is taking place. The ideal power level an amplifier should be capable of producing depends on the efficiency of the speaker and on the level at which you prefer to work, but around 50-250 watts per channel is a reasonable estimate. Amplifiers lower in power than 50 watts can be driven into clipping very easily, especially when used with with less efficient speakers.

That said, I'm a firm believer in using active monitors, as they invariably sound cleaner and more controlled than their passive counterparts. Also, some models include circuitry which protects the speakers from being damaged because of overloading. Active monitors eliminate all of the guesswork involved in buying suitable amplifiers and cabling.

wiring speakers

A speaker cable must have a very low resistance, and the weight of the cable plays a large part in achieving this. However, some people believe that the use of high-purity copper cable will produce a noticeable improvement in the sound quality. Thin wire will compromise the sound of your speakers, but the differences between the sound produced with one good-quality, heavy-duty cable and another are minimal when compared with the differences that can be made by other components in the system. It's true that the capacitance of speaker cable can slightly affect the sound, so it isn't all black magic and marketing, but don't get talked into buying anything too expensive. Speaker cables should be as short as possible, and it's important that both speaker leads are the same length. You should check that the speakers are wired in phase (the red terminal on the amplifier to the red terminal on the speaker) and that the cable ends are firmly clamped at both ends – on the speaker and on the amplifier.

headphones

Headphones can be very useful tools when troubleshooting the monitoring process, but I don't recommend using them as a sole source of monitoring when either mixing or mastering, as the bass response and stereo imaging can sound quite different over loudspeakers. Their bass performance is also affected by the way in which the cushion on the headset seals around the ear, and this is why, when you push the headphones closer to your ears, this produces a noticeable increase in bass. This is a real problem when monitoring, where one of the main aims is to achieve a proper tonal balance across the entire audio spectrum.

Unlike loudspeakers, headphones aren't affected by the acoustics of the room in which they're used, and they convey such detail that it's easy to pick out small noises or distortions that might go unnoticed when heard over monitor speakers.

When a stereo mix is heard over loudspeakers, if the speakers are physically in front of us it's only natural that we hear the soundstage as also being in front of us. With headphones, however, because the sound source is on either side of us there's no front-to-back information for our ears to pick up, and this can produce the illusion that the stereo image is passing through our heads rather than being on a virtual stage in front of the listener.

Furthermore, when listening to stereo material over loudspeakers, some of the sound from the left loudspeaker is picked up by the right ear, and vice versa. In contrast, headphones provide a very high degree of separation between the left and right channels, resulting in an artificially-detailed stereo image. This is a useful characteristic when checking the positions of sounds in the stereo mix, or when checking for recording faults, but the same mix heard over speakers will appear to have not such as wide or clearly-focused stereo spread. Personally speaking, I like to use headphones as an additional stage in the checking process when mastering, because they can show up small faults in material that may be missed when heard over loudspeakers.

open headphones

Open headphones are usually ventilated with slots or holes, to allow sound to pass in and out. In other words, they don't present the same kind of sealed environment as enclosed headphones, but bass performance still varies from model to model depending on how snugly the phone fits over the user's ear. As a rule, the sound heard over a pair of open phones is less coloured than that heard over enclosed phones. In fact, the overall sound quality heard over open headphones can be surprisingly good; they're very good at resolving fine detail and small amounts of distortion, and this makes them ideal for double-checking a mix that may already sound balanced on loudspeakers. For home studio users they are also handy, as they mean that monitoring can be carried out at times when noise might be a problem. Even so, the mix should be checked on loudspeakers before being finally approved.

headphone impedance

Headphone come in a variety of impedances, ranging from eight ohms or so up to several hundred. Most headphone amplifiers will happily drive any impedance they are likely to encounter with no trouble, but if for any reason you wish to split the output from a headphone socket to feed two sets of headphones, you may as well pick phones which have the same impedance, or one set will be louder than the other.

basic acoustic treatments

Good monitors will only sound accurate in a suitable acoustic environment. Without a reliable monitoring room, the mix may sound great in the studio but, as soon as it's played back on another system, the balance may be all wrong, especially at the bass end. If this happens the fault can sometimes be fixed at the mastering stage, but if you're doing your own mastering you need to know that what you're hearing is accurate.

In order to understand the effect the acoustics of a

room can have on the sound, it's important to know exactly what you're actually hearing when you sit down in front of your speakers. Obviously you hear the sound coming directly from the monitor speakers themselves, but this sound energy bounces off every reflective surface in the room, and so there is a significant amount of reflected sound combined with the sound produced by the speakers. This reflected sound arrives at your ears a fraction of a second later than the direct sound, and because some frequencies are absorbed more than others the reflected sound is also coloured.

Some coloration is acceptable, because we are used to living in a moderately reflective acoustic environment, but it must be kept down to a realistic level. One way of achieving this is working in close proximity with the speakers; near-field monitoring offers the advantage that the sound heard by the listener has a greater proportion of the direct sound from the loudspeaker and less sound reflected from the walls, floors and ceilings of the room. It's also true that most untreated rooms perform least accurately at the low bass end of the spectrum, but this problem can be neatly sidestepped by using medium-sized monitors that don't generate extremely low bass. When working with music that relies on extremely deep bass, such as some forms of dance music, it might be sensible to double check mixes over a club sound system or in a professional monitoring environment before manufacturing thousands of CDs. It's also a good idea to check out commercial recordings of a similar style over your monitoring system, which will give you a sense of perspective.

solving room problems

At this point, you should have a pair of decent monitors and, hopefully, an amplifier capable of providing at least as much undistorted power as the speakers can handle. The monitors should be sensibly positioned, behind the console and away from corners of the room, and the engineer's chair should form the apex of an equilateral triangle with the monitors. In a small room, this will often mean setting the speakers up against the longest wall, simply to avoid positioning the speakers too near the corners (and by too close I mean not closer than 18 inches).

flutter echo

Flutter echo is caused by sound bouncing back and forth between two parallel surfaces, which produces an audible ringing. Professional studios are built with walls that aren't parallel, but in a typical home studio parallel walls are usually a fact of life. Fortunately, as you'll be spending most of your time in the engineer's chair, you'll only have to worry about curing any flutter echo that occurs in that position.

The easiest solution to curing flutter echo is to fix a metre-square acoustic foam tile to the wall on each side of the normal listening position and centred at (seated)

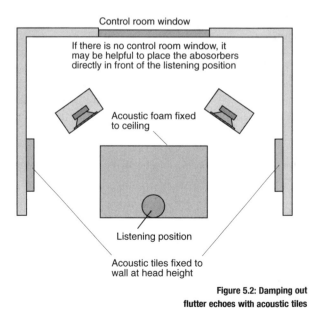

Control room window

If there is no control room window, it may be helpful to place the abosorbers directly in front of the listening position

Acoustic foam fixed to ceiling

Listening position

Acoustic tiles fixed to wall at head height

Figure 5.2: Damping out flutter echoes with acoustic tiles

head height. As well as reducing the flutter echo, this should also noticeably clean up the stereo imaging. Acoustic foam tiles of between two and four inches thickness will work quite well, although a similar thickness of fireproof, open-cell upholstery foam will work almost as well. It's also a good idea to stick a patch of acoustic foam to the ceiling just forward of the listening position, as this will help to tame ceiling reflections. Figure 5.2 depicts a practical monitoring layout, complete with the positions of sound-absorbing tiles to damp out flutter echoes.

rear wall reflections

The last trouble spot is the wall directly behind the desk, because any sound from the monitors that doesn't hit you is going to reflect from this wall and seriously compromise the quality of your monitoring. If the wall is more than ten feet or so behind you then this problem is easily solved. For example, you could position a soft settee along the bottom of the wall and fix a heavy curtain above it, folded into drapes and spaced two or three inches from the wall. Alternatively, you could break up the flat geometry of the wall by fitting shelves for your tapes, manuals, records and CDs. This will help to scatter reflections, although some absorptive material (soft furnishings, for example) is still recommended.

If your studio is in a smaller room, and the back wall is only a few feet behind you, then the ideal solution is to make the wall invisible to audio by turning it into a wide-range acoustic trap. With near-field monitors, it should be enough to fix a six- to eight-inch-deep rockwool slab between battens and cover this with barrier matting (a flexible but heavy mineral-loaded sheet material), and Figure 5.3 illustrates how, by covering the surface of the trap with a layer of fireproof foam, high frequencies can be prevented from bouncing back into the room. However, if you don't want to go to these lengths, it may be enough to hang a heavy curtain over most or all of the rear wall and then fix a row of acoustic foam tiles to the wall at head height, behind the curtain. In most instances, using a

Figure 5.3: A rear wall trap

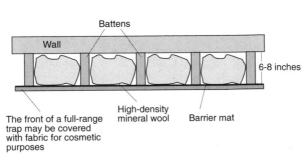

combination of absorbent material and shelving (which acts as a diffusor, scattering reflections) will yield satisfactory results. For more information, there is another book in this series, *basic HOME STUDIO DESIGN*, which covers this area in more detail.

In rooms that are very nearly square, or where the height of the room is similar to the length of one of the walls, peaks in the low-end frequency response are likely to occur because of the action of room modes. A full discussion of room modes is beyond the scope of this book, but basically it means that the room acts as a kind of resonator. The worst case of room modes occurs in a cube-shaped room, where the width, length and height of the room are the same, and the modes produced all occur at the same frequency. In this kind of room, use a layer of absorbent material that's as thick as possible along the back wall and, if possible, in the corners of the room. Choose near-field monitors with a very modest bass response, and work as close to them as is practical.

floors and walls

A wall-to-wall carpet should be fitted if at all possible, which will help to kill floor-to-ceiling reflections (at least at the high end of the audio spectrum, where ringing might be a problem). Heavy felt underlay will also help soundproof the studio and absorb reflections. The entire room should be as symmetrical as possible, not just in the monitoring area, so try and match a reflective surface on one side of the room with a similar surface on the other. If the studio has a window, vertical blinds left half open will significantly reduce high-frequency reflections, and because glass isn't a particularly good isolator of low-frequency sound there also won't be much low-frequency reflection – it'll go straight through.

common cable connections

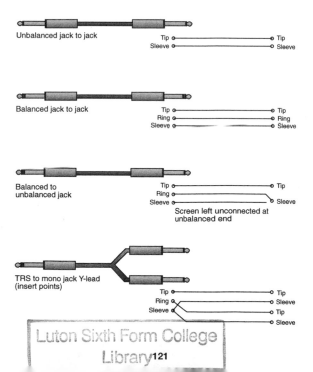

Unbalanced jack to jack

Tip o—————————————o Tip
Sleeve o—————————————o Sleeve

Balanced jack to jack

Tip o—————————————o Tip
Ring o—————————————o Ring
Sleeve o—————————————o Sleeve

Balanced to unbalanced jack

Tip o—————————————o Tip
Ring o—————————————o Sleeve
Sleeve o—————————————o

Screen left unconnected at unbalanced end

TRS to mono jack Y-lead (insert points)

Tip o—————————————o Tip
Ring o—————————————o Sleeve
Sleeve o—————————————o Tip
—————————————o Sleeve

basic mastering

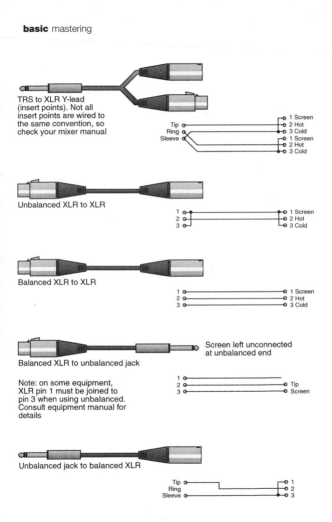

TRS to XLR Y-lead
(insert points). Not all
insert points are wired to
the same convention, so
check your mixer manual

Tip
Ring
Sleeve

1 Screen
2 Hot
3 Cold
1 Screen
2 Hot
3 Cold

Unbalanced XLR to XLR

1
2
3

1 Screen
2 Hot
3 Cold

Balanced XLR to XLR

1
2
3

1 Screen
2 Hot
3 Cold

Balanced XLR to unbalanced jack

Note: on some equipment,
XLR pin 1 must be joined to
pin 3 when using unbalanced.
Consult equipment manual for
details

Screen left unconnected
at unbalanced end

1
2
3

Tip
Screen

Unbalanced jack to balanced XLR

Tip
Ring
Sleeve

1
2
3

122

glossary

AC
Alternating Current.

active
Circuit containing transistors, ICs, tubes and other devices that require power to operate and are capable of amplification.

active sensing
System used to verify that a MIDI connection is working, in which the sending device frequently sends short messages to the receiving device to reassure it that all is well. If these active sensing messages stop for any reason, the receiving device will recognise a fault condition and switch off all notes. Not all MIDI devices support active sensing.

A-to-D converter
Circuit for converting analogue waveforms into a series of values represented by binary numbers. The more bits a converter has the greater the resolution of the sampling process. Current effects units are generally 16 bits or more, with the better models being either 20- or 24-bit.

ADSR
Envelope generator with Attack, Decay, Sustain and Release

parameters. This is a simple type of envelope generator and was first used on early analogue synthesisers, though similar envelopes may be found in some effects units to control filter sweeps and suchlike.

AFL

After-Fade Listen, a system used within mixing consoles to allow specific signals to be monitored at the level set by their fader or level control knob. Aux sends are generally monitored AFL rather than PFL so that the actual signal being fed to an effects unit can be monitored.

aftertouch

Means of generating a control signal based on how much pressure is applied to the keys of a MIDI keyboard. Most instruments that support this do not have independent pressure sensing for all keys but instead detect the overall pressure by means of a sensing strip running beneath the keys. Aftertouch may be used to control musical functions such as vibrato depth, filter brightness, loudness and so on, though it may also be used to control some parameter of a MIDI effects unit, such as delay feedback or effect level.

alpha version

Release version of software which may still contain some bugs (see Beta Version).

algorithm

Computer program designed to perform a specific task. In the context of effects units, algorithms usually describe a software building block designed to create a specific effect or combination of effects. All digital effects are based on algorithms.

aliasing

When an analogue signal is sampled for conversion into a digital data stream, the sampling frequency must be at least twice that of the highest frequency component of the input signal. If this rule is disobeyed, the sampling process becomes ambiguous, as there are insufficient points to define each waveform cycle, resulting in enharmonic sum and difference frequencies being added to the audible signal (see Nyquist Theorem).

ambience

The result of sound reflections in a confined space being added to the original sound. Ambience may also be created electronically by some digital reverb units. The main difference between ambience and reverberation is that ambience doesn't have the characteristic long delay time of reverberation – the reflections mainly give the sound a sense of space.

amp

Unit of electrical current, short for ampere.

amplifier

Device that increases the level of an electrical signal.

amplitude

Another word for level. Can refer to levels of sound or electrical signal.

analogue

Circuitry that uses a continually-changing voltage or current to represent a signal. The origin of the term is that the electrical signal can be thought of as being analogous to the original signal.

anti-aliasing filter
Filter used to limit the frequency range of an analogue signal prior to A/D conversion so that the maximum frequency does not exceed half the sampling rate.

application
Alternative term for computer program.

ASCII
American Standard Code for Information Interchange. A standard code for representing computer keyboard characters with binary data.

attack
Time taken for a sound to achieve maximum amplitude. Drums have a fast attack, whereas bowed strings have a slow attack. In compressors and gates, the attack time equates to how quickly the processor can change its gain.

attenuate
To make lower in level.

audio frequency
Signals in the human audio range, nominally 20Hz-20kHz.

aux
Control on a mixing console designed to route a proportion of the channel signal to the effects or cue mix outputs (see Aux Send).

aux return
Mixer inputs used to add effects to the mix.

aux send
Physical output from a mixer aux send buss.

backup
Safety copy of software or other digital data.

balance
This word has several meanings in recording. It may refer to the relative levels of the left and right channels of a stereo recording, or it may be used to describe the relative levels of the various instruments and voices within a mix.

balanced wiring
Wiring system which uses two out-of-phase conductors and a common screen to reduce the effect of interference. For balancing to be effective, both the sending and receiving device must have balanced output and input stages respectively.

bandpass filter (BDF)
Filter that removes or attenuates frequencies above and below the frequency at which it is set. Frequencies within the band are emphasised. Bandpass filters are often used in synthesisers as tone-shaping elements.

bandwidth
Means of specifying the range of frequencies passed by an electronic circuit such as an amplifier, mixer or filter. The frequency range is usually measured at the points where the level drops by 3dB relative to the maximum.

beta version

Version of software which is not fully tested and may still include bugs.

binary
Counting system based on only two numbers: one and zero.

bios
Part of a computer operating system held on ROM rather than on disk. This handles basic routines such as accessing the disk drive.

bit
Binary digit, which may either be one or zero.

boost/cut control
Single control which allows the range of frequencies passing through a filter to be either amplified or attenuated. The centre position is usually the 'flat' or 'no effect' position.

bouncing
Process of mixing two or more recorded tracks together and re-recording these onto another track.

BPM
Beats Per Minute.

breath controller
Device that converts breath pressure into MIDI controller data.

buffer
Circuit designed to isolate the output of a source device from loading effects due to the input impedance of the

destination device.

buffer memory
Temporary RAM memory used in some computer operations, sometimes to prevent a break in the data stream when the computer is interrupted to perform another task.

bug
Slang term for software fault or equipment design problem.

buss
Common electrical signal path along which signals may travel. In a mixer, there are several busses carrying the stereo mix, the groups, the PFL signal, the aux sends and so on. Power supplies are also fed along busses.

byte
Piece of digital data comprising eight bits.

cardioid
Literally 'heart shaped'. Describes the polar response of a unidirectional microphone.

channel
In the context of MIDI, Channel refers to one of 16 possible data channels over which MIDI data may be sent. The organisation of data by channels means that up to 16 different MIDI instruments or parts may be addressed using a single cable.

channel
In the context of mixing consoles, a channel is a single strip of

controls relating to one input.

chase
Term describing the process whereby a slave device attempts to synchronise itself with a master device. In the context of a MIDI sequence, Chase may also involve chasing events (looking back to earlier positions in the song to see if there are any program changes or other events that need to be acted upon).

chip
Integrated circuit.

chord
Two or more different musical notes played at the same time.

chorus
Effect created by doubling a signal and adding delay and pitch modulation.

chromatic
Describes a scale of pitches rising in steps of one semitone .

click track
Metronome pulse which helps musicians to keep time.

clipping
Severe form of distortion which occurs when a signal attempts to exceed the maximum level which a piece of equipment can handle.

clone

Exact duplicate. Often refers to digital copies of digital tapes.

common-mode rejection
Measure of how well a balanced circuit rejects a signal that is common to both inputs.

compander
Encode/decode device that compresses a signal while encoding it and then expands it when decoding it.

compressor
Device designed to reduce the dynamic range of audio signals by reducing the level of high signals or by increasing the level of low signals.

computer
Device for the storing and processing of digital data.

conductor
Material that provides a low resistance path for electrical current.

console
Alternative term for mixer.

contact enhancer
Compound designed to increase the electrical conductivity of electrical contacts such as plugs, sockets and edge connectors.

continuous controller
Type of MIDI message used to translate continuous change, such as from a pedal, wheel or breath control device.

copy protection
Method used by software manufacturers to prevent unauthorised copying.

crash
Slang term relating to malfunction of a computer program.

cut-and-paste editing
Copying or moving sections of a recording to different locations.

cutoff frequency
Frequency above or below which attenuation begins in a filter circuit.

cycle
One complete vibration of a sound source or its electrical equivalent. One cycle per second is expressed as one Hertz (Hz).

CV
Control Voltage. Used to control the pitch of an oscillator or filter frequency in an analogue synthesiser. Most analogue synthesisers follow a one volt per octave convention, though there are exceptions. To use a pre-MIDI analogue synthesiser under MIDI control, a MIDI-to-CV converter is required.

daisy chain
Term used to describe serial electrical connection between devices or modules.

damping
In the context of reverberation, damping refers to the rate at

which reverberant energy is absorbed by the various surfaces in an environment.

DAT

Digital Audio Tape. The most commonly-used DAT machines are more correctly known as R-DATs because they use a rotating head similar to that in a video recorder. Digital recorders using fixed or stationary heads (such as DCC) are known as S-DAT machines.

data

Information stored and used by a computer.

data compression

System for reducing the amount of data stored by a digital system. Most audio data compression systems are known as lossy systems, because some of the original signal is discarded in accordance with psychoacoustic principles designed to ensure that only components which cannot be heard are lost.

dB

Decibel. Unit used to express the relative levels of two electrical voltages, powers or sounds.

dBm

Variation on dB referenced to 0dB = 1mW into 600ohms.

dBv

Variation on dB referenced to 0dB = 0.775v.

dBV

Variation on dB referenced to 0dB = 1V.

dB/octave

A means of measuring the slope of a filter. The more decibels per octave the sharper the filter slope.

dbx

A commercial encode/decode tape noise reduction system that compresses the signal during recording and expands it by an identical amount on playback.

DC

Direct Current.

DCC

Stationary-head digital recorder format developed by Philips. Uses a data-compression system to reduce the amount of data that needs to be stored.

DCO

Digitally-Controlled Oscillator.

DDL

Digital Delay Line.

decay

Progressive reduction in amplitude of a sound or electrical signal over time. In the context of an ADSR envelope shaper, the decay phase starts as soon as the attack phase has reached its maximum level. In the decay phase, the signal level drops until it reaches the sustain level set by the user. The signal then remains at this level until the key is released, at which point the release phase is entered.

de-esser
Device for reducing the effect of sibilance in vocal signals.

defragmentation
Process of rearranging the files on a hard disk so that all of the files are as contiguous as possible, and that the remaining free space is also contiguous.

deoxidising compound
Substance formulated to remove oxides from electrical contacts.

detent
Physical click stop in the centre of a control such as a pan or EQ cut/boost knob.

DI
Direct Inject, in which a signal is plugged directly into an audio chain without the aid of a microphone.

DI box
Device for matching the signal-level impedance of a source to a tape machine or mixer input.

digital
Electronic system which represents data and signals in the form of codes comprising ones and zeros.

digital delay
Digital processor for generating delay and echo effects.

digital reverb
Digital processor for simulating reverberation.

DIN connector
Consumer multipin signal connection format, also used for MIDI cabling. Various pin configurations are available.

direct coupling
Means of connecting two electrical circuits so that both AC and DC signals may be passed between them.

disc
Used to describe vinyl discs, CDs and MiniDiscs.

disk
Abbreviation of diskette, but now used to describe computer floppy, hard and removable disks (see Floppy Disk).

dither
System of adding low-level noise to a digitised audio signal in a way which extends low-level resolution at the expense of a slight deterioration in noise performance.

DMA
Direct Memory Access. Part of a computer operating system that allows peripheral devices to communicate directly with the computer memory without going via the CPU (Central Processing Unit).

Dolby
An encode/decode tape noise reduction system that amplifies low-level, high-frequency signals during recording,

then reverses this process during playback. There are several different Dolby systems in use, including types B, C and S for domestic and semi-professional machines, and types A and SR for professional machines. Recordings made whilst using one of these systems must also be replayed via the same system.

DOS
Disk Operating System. Part of the operating system of PC and PC-compatible computers.

driver
Piece of software that handles communications between the main program and a hardware peripheral, such as a soundcard, printer or scanner.

drum pad
Synthetic playing surface which produces electronic trigger signals in response to being hit with drumsticks.

dry
Signal to which no effects have been added. Conversely, a sound which has been treated with an effect, such as reverberation, is referred to as wet.

DSP
Digital Signal Processor. A powerful microchip used to process digital signals.

dubbing
Adding further material to an existing recording. Also known as overdubbing.

ducking

System for controlling the level of one audio signal with another. For example, background music can be made to duck whenever there is a voice-over.

dump

To transfer digital data from one device to another. A Sysex dump is a means of transmitting information about a particular instrument or module over MIDI, and may be used to store sound patches, parameter settings and so on.

dynamic microphone

Type of microphone that works on the electric generator principle, whereby a diaphragm moves a coil of wire within a magnetic field.

dynamic range

Range in decibels between the highest signal that can be handled by a piece of equipment and the level at which small signals disappear into the noise floor.

dynamics

Method of describing the relative levels within a piece of music.

early reflections

First sound reflections from walls, floors and ceilings following a sound which is created in an acoustically reflective environment.

effects loop

Connection system that allows an external signal processor to be connected into the audio chain.

effects return

Additional mixer input designed to accommodate the output from an effects unit.

effects unit

Device for treating an audio signal in order to change it in some creative way. Effects often involve the use of delay circuits, and include such treatments as reverb and echo.

encode/decode

System that requires a signal to be processed prior to recording, which is then reversed during playback.

enhancer

Device designed to brighten audio material using techniques such as dynamic equalisation, phase shifting and harmonic generation.

envelope

The way in which the level of a sound or signal varies over time.

envelope generator

Circuit capable of generating a control signal which represents the envelope of the sound you want to recreate. This may then be used to control the level of an oscillator or other sound source, though envelopes may also be used to control filter or modulation settings. The most common example is the ADSR generator.

E-PROM

Similar to ROM, but the information on the chip can be erased and replaced using special equipment.

equaliser
Device for selectively cutting or boosting selected parts of the audio spectrum.

erase
To remove recorded material from an analogue tape, or to remove digital data from any form of storage medium.

event
In MIDI terms, an event is a single unit of MIDI data, such as a note being turned on or off, a piece of controller information, a program change, and so on.

exciter
Enhancer that works by synthesising new high-frequency harmonics.

expander
Device designed to decrease the level of low-level signals and increase the level of high-level signals, thus increasing the dynamic range of the signal.

expander module
Synthesiser with no keyboard, often rack mountable or in some other compact format.

fader
Sliding potentiometer control used in mixers and other processors.

FET
Field Effect Transistor.

figure-of-eight

Describes the polar response of a microphone that is equally sensitive at both front and rear, yet rejects sounds coming from the sides.

file

Meaningful list of data stored in digitally. A Standard MIDI File is a specific type of file designed to allow sequence information to be exchanged between different types of sequencer.

filter

Electronic circuit designed to emphasise or attenuate a specific range of frequencies.

flanging

Modulated delay effect using feedback to create a dramatic, sweeping sound.

floppy disk

Computer disk that uses a flexible magnetic medium encased in a protective plastic sleeve. The maximum capacity of a standard high-density disk is 1.44Mb. Earlier double-density disks hold only around half that amount of data.

flutter echo

Resonant echo that occurs when sound reflects back and forth between two parallel reflective surfaces.

foldback

System for feeding one or more separate mixes to the performers for use while recording and overdubbing. Also known as a cue mix.

formant
Frequency component or resonance of an instrument or voice sound that doesn't change with the pitch of the note being played or sung. For example, the body resonance of an acoustic guitar remains constant regardless of the note being played.

format
Procedure required to ready a computer disk for use. Formatting organises the disk's surface into a series of electronic pigeonholes into which data can be stored. Different computers often use different formatting systems.

fragmentation
Process by which the available space on a disk drive is split up into small sections due to the storing and erasing of files (see Defragmentation).

frequency
Indication of how many cycles of a repetitive waveform occur in one second. A waveform which has a repetition cycle of once per second has a frequency of 1Hz.

frequency response
Measurement of the frequency range that can be handled by a specific piece of electrical equipment or loudspeaker.

FSK
Frequency-Shift Keying. A method of recording a sync clock signal onto tape by representing it as two alternating tones.

fundamental

Any sound comprises a fundamental or basic frequency plus harmonics and partials at a higher frequency.

FX
Shorthand for effects.

gain
Amount by which a circuit amplifies a signal.

gate
Electrical signal that is generated whenever a key is depressed on an electronic keyboard. This is used to trigger envelope generators and other events that need to be synchronised to key action.

gate
Electronic device designed to mute low-level signals, thus improving the noise performance during pauses in the wanted material.

general MIDI
Addition to the basic MIDI spec to assure a minimum level of compatibility when playing back GM-format song files. The specification covers type and program, number of sounds, minimum levels of polyphony and multitimbrality, response to controller information and so on.

glitch
Describes an unwanted short-term corruption of a signal, or the unexplained short-term malfunction of a piece of equipment. For example, an inexplicable click on a DAT tape would be termed a glitch.

GM reset
Universal Sysex command which activates the General MIDI mode on a GM instrument. The same command also sets all controllers to their default values and switches off any notes still playing by means of an All Notes Off message.

graphic equaliser
Equaliser on which several narrow segments of the audio spectrum are controlled by individual cut/boost faders. The name derives from the fact that the fader positions provide a graphic representation of the EQ curve.

ground
Electrical earth, or zero volts. In mains wiring, the ground cable is physically connected to the ground via a long conductive metal spike.

ground loops
Also known as earth loops. Wiring problem in which currents circulate in the ground wiring of an audio system, known as the ground loop effect. When these currents are induced by the alternating mains supply, hum results.

group
Collection of signals within a mixer that are mixed and then routed through a separate fader to provide overall control. In a multitrack mixer, several groups are provided to feed the various recorder track inputs.

GS
An extension to the General MIDI protocol developed by Roland.

hard disk

High-capacity computer storage device based on a rotating rigid disk with a magnetic coating onto which data may be recorded.

harmonic

High-frequency component of a complex waveform.

harmonic distortion

Addition of harmonics not present in the original signal.

head

Part of a tape machine or disk drive that reads and/or writes data to and from the storage media.

headroom

The safety margin in decibels between the highest peak signal being passed by a piece of equipment and the absolute maximum level the equipment can handle.

high-pass filter (HPF)

Filter which attenuates frequencies below its cutoff frequency.

hiss

Noise caused by random electrical fluctuations.

hum

Signal contamination caused by the addition of low frequencies, usually related to the mains power frequency.

Hz

Shorthand for Hertz, the unit of frequency.

IC
Integrated Circuit.

impedance
Can be visualised as the AC resistance of a circuit which contains both resistive and reactive components.

inductor
Reactive component which presents an impedance with increases with frequency.

initialise
To automatically restore a piece of equipment to its factory default settings.

insert point
Connector that allows an external processor to be patched into a signal path so that the signal then flows through the external processor.

insulator
Material that does not conduct electricity.

interface
Device that acts as an intermediary to two or more other pieces of equipment. For example, a MIDI interface enables a computer to communicate with MIDI instruments and keyboards.

intermittent
Usually describes a fault that only appears occasionally.

intermodulation distortion

Form of distortion that introduces frequencies not present in the original signal. These are invariably based on the sum and difference products of the original frequencies.

I/O
The part of a system that handles inputs and outputs, usually in the digital domain.

IPS
Inches Per Second. Used to describe tape speed.

IRQ
Interrupt Request. Part of the operating system of a computer that allows a connected device to request attention from the processor in order to transfer data to it or from it.

isopropyl alcohol
Type of alcohol commonly used for cleaning and de-greasing tape machine heads and guides.

jack
Commonly audio connector. May be mono (TS) or stereo (TRS).

jargon
Specialised words associated with a specialist subject.

k
Abbreviation for 1000 (kilo). Used as a prefix to other values to indicate magnitude.

kHz
1000Hz.

kohm
1000 ohms.

LCD
Liquid Crystal Display.

LED
Light-Emitting Diode. Solid-state lamp.

LSB
Least Significant Byte. If a piece of data has to be conveyed as two bytes, one byte represents high-value numbers and the other low-value numbers, in much the same way as tens and units function in the decimal system. The high value, or most significant part of the message, is called the Most Significant Byte or MSB.

limiter
Device that controls the gain of a signal, in order to prevent it from ever exceeding a level preset by the user. A limiter is essentially a fast-acting compressor with an infinite compression ratio.

linear
Device where the output is a direct multiple of the input.

line level
Mixers and signal processors tend to work at a standard signal level known as line level. In practice there are several different standard line levels, but all are in the order of a few volts. A nominal signal level is around -10dBv for semi-pro equipment and +4dBv for professional equipment.

load

Electrical circuit that draws power from another circuit or power supply. Also a verb, describing reading data into a computer.

load on/off

Function to allow the keyboard and sound-generating section of a keyboard synthesiser to be used independently of each other.

logic

Type of electronic circuitry used for processing binary signals comprising two discrete voltage levels.

loop

Circuit where the output is connected back to the input.

low-frequency oscillator (LFO)

Oscillator used as a modulation source, usually below 20Hz. The most common LFO waveshape is the sine wave, though there is often a choice of sine, square, triangular and sawtooth waveforms.

low-pass filter (LPF)

A filter which attenuates frequencies above its cutoff frequency.

mA

Milliamp, or one thousandth of an amp.

MDM

Modular Digital Multitrack. A digital recorder that can be used in multiples to provide a greater number of synchronised tracks than a single machine.

meg
Abbreviation for the prefix mega (1,000,000).

memory
Computer's RAM memory used to store programs and data. This data is lost when the computer is switched off and so must be stored to disk or other suitable media.

menu
List of choices presented by a computer program or a device with a display window.

mic level
Low-level signal generated by a microphone. This must be amplified many times to increase it to line level.

microprocessor
Specialised microchip at the heart of a computer. It is here that instructions are read and acted upon.

MIDI
Musical Instrument Digital Interface.

MIDI analyser
Device that gives a visual readout of MIDI activity when connected between two pieces of MIDI equipment.

MIDI bank change
Type of controller message used to select alternate banks of MIDI programs where access to more than 128 programs is required.

MIDI controller

Term used to describe the physical interface by means of which the musician plays the MIDI synthesiser or other sound generator. Examples of controllers are keyboards, drum pads, wind synths and so on.

MIDI control change

Also known as MIDI Controllers or Controller Data. These messages convey positional information relating to performance controls such as wheels, pedals, switches and other devices. This information can be used to control functions such as vibrato depth, brightness, portamento, effects levels, and many other parameters.

(standard) MIDI file

Standard file format for storing song data recorded on a MIDI sequencer in such as way as to allow it to be read by other makes or models of MIDI sequencer.

MIDI implementation chart

A chart, usually found in MIDI product manuals, which provides information as to which MIDI features are supported. Supported features are marked with a 0 while unsupported feature are marked with a X. Additional information may be provided, such as the exact form of the bank change message.

MIDI in

The socket used to receive information from a master controller or from the MIDI Thru socket of a slave unit.

MIDI merge

Device or sequencer function that enables two or more

streams of MIDI data to be combined.

MIDI mode

MIDI information can be interpreted by the receiving MIDI instrument in a number of ways, the most common being polyphonically on a single MIDI channel (poly-omni off mode). Omni mode enables a MIDI Instrument to play all incoming data regardless of channel.

MIDI module

Sound-generating device with no integral keyboard.

MIDI note number

Every key on a MIDI keyboard has its own note number, ranging from 0 to 127, where 60 represents middle C. Some systems use C3 as middle C while others use C4.

MIDI note off

MIDI message sent when key is released.

MIDI note on

Message sent when note is pressed.

MIDI out

MIDI connector used to send data from a master device to the MIDI In of a connected slave device.

MIDI port

MIDI connections of a MIDI-compatible device. A multiport, in the context of a MIDI interface, is a device with multiple MIDI output sockets, each capable of carrying data relating to a different set of 16 MIDI channels. Multiports are the only means of exceeding the limitations imposed by 16 MIDI channels.

MIDI program change
Type of MIDI message used to change sound patches on a remote module or the effects patch on a MIDI effects unit.

MIDI splitter
Alternative term for MIDI thru box.

MIDI sync
Description of the synchronisation systems available to MIDI users: MIDI Clock and MIDI Time Code.

MIDI thru
Socket on a slave unit used to feed the MIDI In socket of the next unit in line.

MIDI thru box
Device which splits the MIDI Out signal of a master instrument or sequencer to avoid daisy chaining. Powered circuitry is used to 'buffer' the outputs so as to prevent problems when many pieces of equipment are driven from a single MIDI output.

mixer
Device for combining two or more audio signals.

monitor
Reference loudspeaker used for mixing.

monitor
VDU for a computer.

monitoring
Action of listening to a mix or a specific audio signal.

monophonic
One note at a time.

motherboard
Main circuit board within a computer into which all the other components plug or connect.

MTC
MIDI Time Code. A MIDI sync implementation based on SMPTE time code.

multisample
Creation of several samples, each covering a limited musical range, the idea being to produce a more natural range of sounds across the range of the instrument being sampled. For example, a piano may need to be sampled every two or three semitones in order to sound convincing.

multitimbral module
MIDI sound source capable of producing several different sounds at the same time and controlled on different MIDI channels.

multitrack
Recording device capable of recording several 'parallel' parts or tracks which may then be mixed or re-recorded independently.

near field

Some people prefer the term 'close field' to describe a loudspeaker system designed to be used close to the listener. The advantage is that the listener hears more of the direct sound from the speakers and less of the reflected sound from the room.

noise reduction
System for reducing analogue tape noise or for reducing the level of hiss present in a recording.

noise shaping
System for creating digital dither so that any added noise is shifted into those parts of the audio spectrum where the human ear is least sensitive.

non-linear recording
Describes digital recording systems that allow any parts of the recording to be played back in any order with no gaps. Conventional tape is referred to as linear, because the material can only play back in the order in which it was recorded.

non-registered parameter number
Addition to the basic MIDI spec that allows controllers 98 and 99 to be used to control non-standard parameters relating to particular models of synthesiser. This is an alternative to using system-exclusive data to achieve the same ends, though NRPNs tend to be used mainly by Yamaha and Roland instruments.

normalise
A socket is said to be normalised when it is wired such that the original signal path is maintained, unless a plug is inserted into

the socket. The most common examples of normalised connectors are the insert points on a mixing console.

nut
Slotted plastic or bone component at the headstock end of a guitar neck used to guide the strings over the fingerboard, and to space the strings above the frets.

Nyquist theorem
The rule which states that a digital sampling system must have a sample rate at least twice as high as that of the highest frequency being sampled in order to avoid aliasing. Because anti-aliasing filters aren't perfect, the sampling frequency usually has to be made more than twice that of the maximum input frequency.

octave
When a frequency or pitch is transposed up by one octave, its frequency is doubled.

off-line
Process carried out while a recording is not playing. For example, some computer-based processes have to be carried out off-line as the computer isn't fast enough to carry out the process in real time.

ohm
Unit of electrical resistance.

omni
Refers to a microphone that is equally sensitive in all directions, or to the MIDI mode in which data on all channels is recognised.

open circuit
Break in an electrical circuit that prevents current from flowing.

open reel
Tape machine on which the tape is wound on spools rather than sealed in a cassette.

operating system
Basic software that enables a computer to load and run other programs.

opto-electronic device
Device on which some electrical parameters change in response to a variation in light intensity. Variable photoresistors are sometimes used as gain control elements in compressors where the side-chain signal modulates the light intensity.

oscillator
Circuit designed to generate a periodic electrical waveform.

overdub
To add another part to a multitrack recording or to replace one of the existing parts (see Dubbing).

overload
To exceed the operating capacity of an electronic or electrical circuit.

pad
Resistive circuit for reducing signal level.

pan pot

Control enabling the user of a mixer to move the signal to any point in the stereo soundstage by varying the relative levels fed to the left and right stereo outputs.

parallel

Method of connecting two or more circuits together so that their inputs and outputs are all connected together.

parameter

Variable value that affects some aspect of a device's performance.

parametric EQ

Equaliser with separate controls for frequency, bandwidth and cut/boost.

passive

Circuit with no active elements.

patch

Alternative term for program. Referring to a single programmed sound within a synthesiser that can be called up using program-change commands. MIDI effects units and samplers also have patches.

patch bay

System of panel-mounted connectors used to bring inputs and outputs to a central point from where they can be routed using plug-in patch cords.

patch cord

Short cable used with patch bays.

peak
Maximum instantaneous level of a signal.

peak
The highest signal level in any section of programme material.

PFL
Pre-Fade Listen. A system used within a mixing console to allow the operator to listen in on a selected signal, regardless of the position of the fader currently controlling that signal.

phantom power
48v DC supply for capacitor microphones, transmitted along the signal cores of a balanced mic cable.

phase
Timing difference between two electrical waveforms expressed in degrees where 360° corresponds to a delay of exactly one cycle.

phaser
Effect which combines a signal with a phase-shifted version of itself to produce creative filtering effects. Most phasers are controlled by means of an LFO.

phono plug
Hi-fi connector developed by RCA and used extensively on semi-pro, unbalanced recording equipment.

pickup
Part of a guitar that converts string vibrations to electrical signals.

pitch
Musical interpretation of an audio frequency.

pitch bend
Special control message specifically designed to produce a change in pitch in response to the movement of a pitch bend wheel or lever. Pitch bend data can be recorded and edited, just like any other MIDI controller data, even though it isn't part of the controller message group.

pitch shifter
Device for changing the pitch of an audio signal without changing its duration.

polyphony
An instrument's ability to play two or more notes simultaneously. An instrument which can play only one note at a time is described as monophonic.

poly mode
The most common MIDI mode, which allows any instrument to respond to multiple simultaneous notes transmitted on a single MIDI channel.

port
Connection for the input or output of data.

portamento

Gliding effect that allows a sound to change pitch at a gradual rate rather than abruptly when a new key is pressed or MIDI note sent.

post-production
Work done to a stereo recording after mixing has been completed.

post-fade
Aux signal taken from after the channel fader so that the aux send level follows any channel fader changes. Normally used for feeding effects devices.

power supply
Unit designed to convert mains electricity to the voltages necessary to power an electronic circuit or device.

PPM
Peak Programme Meter. A meter designed to register signal peaks rather than the average level.

PPQN
Pulsed Per Quarter Note. Used in the context of MIDI clock-derived sync signals.

PQ coding
Process for adding pause, cue and other subcode information to a digital master tape in preparation for CD manufacture.

pre-emphasis
System for applying high-frequency boost to a sound before processing so as to reduce the effect of noise. A corresponding

de-emphasis process is required on playback so as to restore the original signal and to attenuate any high-frequency noise contributed by the recording process.

pre-fade
Aux signal taken from before the channel fader so that the channel fader has no effect on the aux send level. Normally used for creating foldback or cue mixes.

preset
Effects unit or synth patch that cannot be altered by the user.

pressure
Alternative term for aftertouch.

print through
Undesirable process that causes some magnetic information from a recorded analogue tape to become imprinted onto an adjacent layer. This can produce low-level pre- or post-echoes.

processor
Device designed to treat an audio signal by changing its dynamics or frequency content. Examples of processors include compressors, gates and equalisers.

program change
MIDI message designed to change instrument or effects unit patches.

pulse wave

Similar to a square wave but non-symmetrical. Pulse waves sound brighter and thinner than their square counterparts, making them useful in the synthesis of reed instruments. The timbre changes according to the mark/space ratio of the waveform.

pulse-width modulation

Means of modulating the duty cycle (mark/space ratio) of a pulse wave. This changes the timbre of the basic tone. LFO modulation of pulse width can be used to produce a pseudo-chorus effect.

punch-in

Action of placing an already recorded track into record at the correct time during playback so that the existing material may be extended or replaced.

punch-out

Action of switching a tape machine (or other recording device) out of record after executing a punch in. With most multitrack machines, both punching in and punching out can be accomplished without stopping the tape.

PZM

Pressure Zone Microphone. A type of boundary microphone, designed to reject out-of-phase sounds reflected from surfaces within the recording environment.

Q

Measurement of the resonant properties of a filter. The higher the Q, the more resonant the filter and the narrower the range of frequencies that are allowed to pass.

quantising

Means of moving notes recorded in a MIDI sequencer so that they line up with user defined subdivisions of a musical bar – 16s, for example. The facility may be used to correct timing errors, but over-quantising can remove the human feel from a performance.

RAM

Abbreviation for Random Access Memory. This is a type of memory used by computers for the temporary storage of programs and data, and all data is lost when the power is turned off. For that reason, work needs to be saved to disk if it is not to be lost.

R-DAT

Digital tape machine using a rotating head system.

real time

Audio process that can be carried out as the signal is being recorded or played back. The opposite is off-line, where the signal is processed in non-real time.

release

Time taken for a level or gain to return to normal. Often used to describe the rate at which a synthesised sound reduces in level after a key has been released.

resistance

Opposition to the flow of electrical current. Measured in ohms.

resolution

Accuracy with which an analogue signal is represented by a digitising system. The more bits are used, the more accurately the amplitude of each sample can be measured, but there are other elements of converter design that also affect accuracy. High conversion accuracy is known as high resolution.

resonance
Same as Q.

reverb
Acoustic ambience created by multiple reflections in a confined space.

RF
Radio Frequency.

RF interference
Interference significantly above the range of human hearing.

ribbon microphone
Microphone in which the sound-capturing element is a thin metal ribbon suspended in a magnetic filed. When sound causes the ribbon to vibrate, a small electrical current is generated within the ribbon.

ring modulator
Device that accepts and processes two input signals in a particular way. The output signal does not contain any of the original input signal but instead comprises new frequencies based on the sum and difference of the input signal's frequency components. The best-known application of ring modulation is the creation of Dalek voices, but it may also be

used to create dramatic instrumental textures. Depending on the relationships between the input signals, the results may either be musical or extremely dissonant – for example, ring modulation can be used to create bell-like tones. (The term 'ring' is used because the original circuit which produced the effect used a ring of diodes.)

RMS
Root Mean Square. A method of specifying the behaviour of a piece of electrical equipment under continuous sine wave testing conditions.

roll-off
The rate at which a filter attenuates a signal once it has passed the filter cutoff point.

ROM
Abbreviation for Read-Only Memory. This is a permanent and non-volatile type of memory containing data that can't be changed. Operating systems are often stored on ROM as the memory remains intact when the power is switched off.

safety copy
Copy or clone of an original tape for use in case of loss of or damage to the original.

sample
Process carried out by an A/D converter where the instantaneous amplitude of a signal is measured many times per second (44.1kHz in the case of CD).

sample

Digitised sound used as a musical sound source in a sampler or additive synthesiser.

sample and hold

Usually refers to a feature whereby random values are generated at regular intervals and then used to control another function such as pitch or filter frequency. Sample and hold circuits were also used in old analogue synthesisers to 'remember' the note being played after a key had been released.

sample rate

Number of times which an A-to-D converter samples the incoming waveform each second.

sawtooth wave

So called because it resembles the teeth of a saw, this waveform contains only even harmonics.

SCSI

(Pronounced 'skuzzi'.) Small Computer System Interface. An interfacing system for using hard drives, scanners, CD-ROM drives and similar peripherals with a computer. Each SCSI device has its own ID number and no two SCSI devices in the same chain must be set to the same number. The last SCSI device in the chain should be terminated either via an internal terminator, where provided, or via a plug-in terminator fitted to a free SCSI socket.

sequencer

Device for recording and replaying MIDI data, usually in a multitrack format, allowing complex compositions to be built up a part at a time.

short circuit

Low-resistance path that allows electrical current to flow. The term is usually used to describe a current path that exists through a faulty condition.

sibilance

High-frequency whistling or lisping sound that affects vocal recordings due either to poor mic technique or excessive equalisation.

side chain

Part of a circuit that splits off a proportion of the main signal to be processed in some way. Compressors use a side-chain signal to derive their control signals.

signal

Electrical representation of input such as sound.

signal chain

Route taken by a signal from the input of a system to its output.

signal-to-noise ratio

Ratio of maximum signal level to the residual noise, expressed in decibels.

sine wave

Waveform of a pure tone with no harmonics.

single-ended noise reduction

Device for removing or attenuating the noise component of a signal. Doesn't require previous coding, as in the case of Dolby or dbx.

slave
Device under the control of a master device.

SMPTE
Time code developed for the film industry but now extensively used in music and recording. SMPTE is a real-time code and is related to hours, minutes, seconds and film or video frames rather than to musical tempo.

SPL
Sound-Pressure Level. Measured in decibels.

SPP
Song-Position Pointer (MIDI).

standard MIDI file
Standard file format that allows MIDI files to be transferred between different sequencers and MIDI file players.

step time
System for programming a sequencer in non-real time.

stereo
Two-channel system feeding left and right loudspeakers.

stripe
To record time code onto one track of a multitrack tape machine.

square wave

Symmetrical rectangular waveform. Square waves contain a series of odd harmonics.

sub-bass

Frequencies below the range of typical monitor loudspeakers. Some define sub-bass as frequencies that can be felt rather than heard.

subcode

Hidden data embedded within the CD and DAT format that includes such information as the absolute time location, number of tracks, total running time of the CD or tape and so on.

subtractive synthesis

Process of creating a new sound by filtering and shaping a raw, harmonically complex waveform.

surge

Sudden increase in mains voltage.

sustain

Part of the ADSR envelope which determines the level to which the sound will settle if a key is held down. Once the key is released, the sound decays at a rate set by the release parameter. Also refers to a guitar's ability to hold notes which decay very slowly.

sweet spot

Optimum position for a microphone or a listener relative to monitor loudspeakers.

switching power supply

Type of power supply that uses a high-frequency oscillator prior to the transformer so that a smaller, lighter transformer may be used. These power supplies are commonly used in computers and some synthesiser modules.

sync

System for making two or more pieces of equipment run in synchronism with each other.

synthesiser

Electronic musical instrument designed to create a wide range of sounds, both imitative and abstract.

tape head

Part of a tape machine that transfers magnetic energy to the tape during recording or reads it during playback.

tempo

Rate of the beat of a piece of music, measured here in beats per minute.

test tone

Steady, fixed-level tone recorded onto a multitrack or stereo recording to act as a reference when matching levels.

THD

Total Harmonic Distortion.

thru

MIDI connector which passes on the signal received at the MIDI In socket.

timbre

Tonal 'colour' of a sound.

track

This term dates back to multitrack tape, on which the tracks are physical stripes of recorded material located side by side along the length of the tape.

tracking

System whereby one device follows another. Tracking is often discussed in the context of MIDI guitar synthesisers or controllers where the MIDI output attempts to track the pitch of the guitar strings.

transducer

Device for converting one form of energy into another. A microphone is a good example of a transducer, as it converts mechanical energy to electrical energy.

transparency

Subjective term used to describe audio quality where the high-frequency detail is clear and individual sounds are easy to identify and separate.

transpose

To shift a musical signal by a fixed number of semitones.

tremolo

Modulation of the amplitude of a sound using an LFO.

triangle wave

Symmetrical, triangle-shaped wave containing only odd

harmonics, but with a lower harmonic content than the square wave.

TRS jack
Stereo-type jack with tip, ring and sleeve connections.

unbalanced
Two-wire electrical signal connection where the inner (or hot, or positive) conductor is usually surrounded by the outer (or cold, or negative) conductor, forming a screen against interference.

unison
To play the same melody using two or more different instruments or voices.

valve
Vacuum-tube amplification component, also known as a tube.

velocity
The rate at which a key is depressed. This may be used to control loudness (to simulate the response of instruments such as pianos) or other parameters on later synthesisers.

vibrato
Pitch modulation using an LFO to modulate a VCO.

vocoder
Signal processor that imposes a changing spectral filter on a sound based on the frequency characteristics of a second sound. By taking the spectral content of a human voice and

imposing it on a musical instrument, talking instrument effects can be created.

voice

Capacity of a synthesiser to play a single musical note. An instrument capable of playing 16 simultaneous notes is said to be a 16-voice instrument.

volt

Unit of electrical power.

VU meter

Meter designed to interpret signal levels in roughly the same way as the human ear, which responds more closely to the average levels of sounds rather than to the peak levels.

wah pedal

Guitar effects device where a bandpass filter is varied in frequency by means of a pedal control.

warmth

Subjective term used to describe sound where the bass and low mid frequencies have depth and where the high frequencies are smooth sounding rather than being aggressive or fatiguing. Warm-sounding tube equipment may also exhibit some of the aspects of compression.

watt

Unit of electrical power.

waveform

Graphic representation of the way in which a sound wave or

electrical wave varies with time.

white noise
Random signal with an energy distribution that produces the same amount of noise power per Hz.

write
To save data to a digital storage medium, such as a hard drive.

XG
Yamaha's alternative to Roland's GS system for enhancing the General MIDI protocol so as to provide additional banks of patches and further editing facilities.

XLR
Type of connector commonly used to carry balanced audio signals, including the feeds from microphones.

Y-lead
Lead split so that one source can feed two destinations. Y-leads may also be used in console insert points, when a stereo jack plug at one end of the lead is split into two monos at the other.

zero crossing point
Point at which a signal waveform crosses from being positive to negative and vice versa.

zipper noise
Audible steps that occur when a parameter is being varied in a digital audio processor.